Prais

Trig

"*Triggers* is a powerful book about helping you maintain emotional control as a parent so that you can be most effective. Wendy and Amber leave you feeling hopeful because of their practical advice, convicted because of their biblical insight, and inspired because of their ability to relate with story after story. You'll fall in love with this book while it changes your heart!"

— Dr. Scott Turansky, National Center for Biblical Parenting

"Nothing has caught me more off guard than the anger I have experienced in parenting young kids. When my boys were little, I cried out to God and read every book I could find for help in overcoming my mommy-anger issues. *Triggers* would have been life changing for me back then, as it is so spot-on in speaking to the very universal triggers for anger in parenting, and then offers the most gracious and practical help for each one. Now, I urge all parents to open this book daily, whether you are overcoming an anger habit or because you want to be proactive against one!"

— Monica Swanson, author of *The Secret of Your Naturally Skinny Friends*, and the popular blog, MonicaSwanson.com

"God used *Triggers* to reveal cracks in my parenting. This series has helped me not only identify triggers in my life, but it also provided me with truth and grace from God's Word to correct, teach, and empower me as a mom.

— Laura Mitchell, author of the blog, LivingInFreedomEveryDay.blogspot.com

"Every mom needs this! If you're just getting started with your family or facing an empty nest, *Triggers* will inspire you to take an honest, biblical look at in the mirror. You'll love the stories, the honesty, and the strength of hope this book offers. It's a good, strong cup of coffee when your heart is worn out."

— Lisa Pennington, Texas mom of 9, author of *Mama Needs a Do-Over: Simple Steps for Turning a Hard Day Around,* and writer at ThePenningtonPoint.com

"Thank you Wendy and Amber for thoughtfully and honestly addressing numerous issues that set us off, and then pointing us to a better way through God's Word. Bringing these triggers to light empowers us to move forward as kinder, wiser, and better-equipped moms."

— Katie M. Reid, author of the blog, KatieMReid.com

"I'm an author and a speaker. I write blogs and books on parenting topics, and I know how to give good advice. I'm also a mom of 10 children, and there have been many times I've thought, "I'm so glad my audience didn't just see me/hear that!" There are times my patience impresses even myself, but there are also times when my voice raises, my emotions flair, and I'm too loud, too firm, too out of control. I hurt my children. I also poorly reflect my Heavenly Father. *Triggers* is a book for every mom, but especially for me. The book looks beyond the outward displays to the heart of the matter. I was inspired and encouraged by this book! It's a must-read for every mom who struggles with anger...which means all of us!"

— Tricia Goyer, USA Today best-selling author of 50 books, including *Balanced: Finding Center as A Work-at-Home Mom*

What moms are saying about

Triggers

"Day by day, trigger by trigger, God is showing me where I have relied on my own strength and emotional reactions rather than His strength and right biblical responses. *Triggers* is helping me become the mom I want to be."

— Brandi J., Ontario

"*Triggers* has been life-changing for me. It not only opened my eyes to the things that were causing me to lose it, but it also showed me I wasn't the only mom struggling. I found hope, healing, and some awesome biblical guidance. Before reading *Triggers*, I used to cry my eyes out, repenting for my sinful anger, and hoping for a change. Now, I have tools to really change my responses, and handle situations more lovingly—more like Christ."

— Christine M., Arizona

"*Triggers* reminded me that children misbehave—but I don't have to. It's my choice in how I respond as I give myself to the guidance of the Holy Spirit."

— Shonda K., Washington

"Had you told me years ago that one of my biggest struggles as a mom would be dealing with anger, I would never have believed you. This book first helped me come to the realization that I have triggers for that anger. More importantly, I have been encouraged and challenged by the practical, biblical tools given.

— Jana H., Hungary

Triggers

EXCHANGING PARENTS' ANGRY REACTIONS
FOR GENTLE BIBLICAL RESPONSES

•••

AMBER LIA AND WENDY SPEAKE

PUBLISHED BY SAME PAGE PRESS

Cover by Alle McCloskey, Finding Eden Media, Ohio
Cover Photo by Prixel Creative
Edited by Nate McCloskey, Finding Eden Media, Ohio
Page Design and Layout by Alle McCloskey, Finding Eden Media, Ohio

• •

Triggers is dedicated to the sons and daughters of every mom who reads this book and prays for the Holy Spirit to transform her heart and home, dramatically changing their family's spiritual legacy. We pray for generations of blessing upon you and your children, and your children's children—until the day of Christ's return.

With Him, this is possible!

• •

CONTENTS

•••

INTRODUCTION

•••

Looking into the sweet, tiny faces of our newborn babies, we never would have imagined the day we would morph into exasperated moms who wound with words and grapple with guilt. For many of us, our anger catches us off guard, slowly building and exploding over whatever final straw has added to the stress, helplessness, and feelings of inadequacy that trigger our anger. For others, we should have known. Our childhoods were a series of angry encounters and we are simply living out what was modeled for us. But for every brave mom who is willing to admit she has a problem with anger or yelling, there are hundreds more who wonder if they are the only ones who struggle.

You are certainly not alone in your battle for peace and grace in your home. If you have picked up this book, then you are one among many thousands of moms who feel stuck in the turbulent tug-of-war of emotions that anger brings into your mothering.

Is there hope for change?

Are you a candidate to become a grace-filled mom whose children will one day rise up to bless?

Can you grow spiritually so that love rules and you breathe life-giving words into your kids?

Will you ever stop being afraid that you are harming your kids beyond repair?

Is there a better way, and will you be able to master it?

Absolutely. Moms, you can take your mothering from heated to holy.

Here's how I know:

When the idea of starting an online support group for moms who struggle with anger and yelling was presented to me, I didn't jump at the chance. I had no problem admitting that I was, indeed, a recovering angry mom; it's just that I spent my growing up years pulsated by the anger of others, and I spent many years sorting through and healing from those banged-up emotions. I wasn't in a big hurry to revisit it. But the Holy Spirit prodded my reluctant heart, so I raised my hand after all.

I had no idea that we would swell to thousands upon thousands of amazing moms in a matter of months. One thing is crystal clear: there is a need for someone to offer an alternative to quick-tempered reactionary parenting. Women all over the world are desperate for practical help and biblical truth.

Eventually, my friend and fellow author, Wendy Speake, was nudged to join me in this ministry. She's a mom who knows a thing or two about tender parenting, living it out every day in her own home with three kids. Wendy and I come from different backgrounds and family dynamics with our own children, so our unique trials and tests as moms have equipped us to offer insights and encouragement that complement one another. We want to offer all of that to you.

We wrote this book—this collection of 31 anger triggers and how to respond to them biblically—because we know that there is a godly way to handle the situations that light us up and set us off. Wendy and I are passionate about encouraging moms who want to live in freedom, not shackled to anger. In each of the 31 days of triggers, we talk about everything, from managing the exhaustion we feel as mothers; to toddler meltdowns and back-talking preteens; to handling the pressures of multi-tasking and caring for kids with special needs.

The chapters are short enough for busy moms to read one a day for an entire month—a devotional that, if applied and prayed over, will radically transform your thinking and begin to bring about lasting change. This book began as a series in our online support group and we quickly saw the overwhelmingly positive response of walking through common anger triggers, practically and biblically. Our ministry has been going strong for more than a year now, and we treasure every testimony of victory and freedom from anger. It works because when we apply truth to our hearts, the Holy Spirit does all the work and God gets all the glory. Now, it's your turn to ditch the anger for good.

Read a chapter a day, prayerfully. Expectantly.

You can count on God's promise that He "is able to do immeasurably more than all we ask or imagine, according to his power that is at work within us" (Ephesians 3:20). Dream big. Let yourself imagine a home where your words set a tone of loving-kindness. A home where your first reaction is compassion instead of annoyance. Where you replace the fiery cycle of anger and guilt with conviction and spiritual growth. A place where you draw the hearts of your children towards grace and where every one of you thrives.

With Love,

Amber

SECTION ONE:
EXTERNAL TRIGGERS

WHEN IT HAS EVERYTHING TO DO WITH THEM...

Here at the beginning of journey together, we are jumping straight into the most common things our children do in their childishness that drive us crazy and make us angry. From talking back and ignoring our instructions to angry fits and whining meltdowns. All of the things "they should have learned by now" but haven't; those are the triggers we're focusing on here in section one.

CHAPTER 1: DISOBEDIENCE

I stood in my high heels and pencil skirt, cheering wildly as students ran laps around the dusty track. Stacey was among them. She was my tenth-grade English student, whom I was also mentoring in a small group Bible study after school. Stacey had a lot of emotional problems and she often felt like a failure. Her mom worried and asked me to watch out for her daughter. For the last two years, Stacey had tried to pass her Presidential Fitness Test in Physical Education, but she simply couldn't do it. The year I had her in my class, I knew it was Providence that allowed her P.E. class to coincide with my break period, and I made way to the field on testing day.

I could tell she was petering out as the last few laps loomed.

I took off my heels and began to run alongside her, "You can do this, Stacey! I know it! Only 3 more laps to go! Don't give up!" I watched as her weary face took on more confidence and her pace quickened...

Much like Stacey's race, parenting is anything but easy. I have heard from countless moms over the years who become incensed by disobedient kids. It seems like every new day brings with it a new battle. We could look at hundreds of different parenting styles and approaches to try and teach our kids to obey us. I could list lots of techniques and tricks to turn your child from combative to compliant and some of them just might work. But what might be missing personally in our quest for obedient kids?

We may very well miss an opportunity to become more like Christ *ourselves*.

When our kids disobey us, we often resort to unrighteous anger. We yell. We put our hands on our hips and scowl unbecomingly. Swift punishment follows on the heels of a stern lecture. Sometimes, we simultaneously know that we are doing more harm than good, but we can't seem to stop ourselves. We feel at a loss for a better way to get through to our children.

God is clear in His Word about obedience:

> *"Children, obey your parents in the Lord, for this is right." Ephesians 6:1*

> *"Honor your father and your mother, that you may live a long time in the land the Lord your God is giving to you." Exodus 20:12, NET*

> *"Children, obey your parents in everything, for this pleases the Lord." Colossians 3:20*

God wants us to obey because obedience gives birth to blessings. We will always be the better for it when we obey the first time. I have heard others say that if our kids don't obey immediately, then we must punish them immediately. And yet, time and time again in Scripture, we see the long-suffering and compassion of God toward His stubborn and wayward people.

He is the God of 70 times 7 chances.

He doesn't whack us upside the head continually or deal harshly with us from the get-go.

He reminds us to go and sin no more and He leaves us to it.

No more condemnation.

He goes so far as to cover our sin with His love, and when we misuse and abuse our freedom, staggering home from our prodigal mess, He throws us a party, rejoicing over our repentance.

God is not cookie cutter, yet His character is consistent.

As parents we can camp out on a few select verses about justice and discipline, establishing a rigid routine for discipline. However, I see far more biblical evidence throughout both the Old and New Testaments that supports an overarching attitude and character of patience, mercy, kindness, and grace extended towards us from a Holy God who loves us and gave Himself for us.

Even while we were yet sinners.

Even when we were enemies.

Even when we reviled Him as He died on the cross for our sins.

And in my own life, I'm so thankful God didn't treat me as my sins deserved —when I dated the wrong guys, or held a grudge against a friend,

IRON FISTS CHISEL STONY HEARTS, BUT GRACEFUL HANDS SHAPE RESPONSIVE HEARTS.

or yelled at my own kids as a young mom. I missed out on blessings by my disobedience, for sure. But God, in His grace, drew me with His loving-kindness over and over and over again. Proverbs 10:12 reminds us, "Hatred stirs up strife, but love covers all offenses."

As mothers, we forget that our kids are immature. Yes, they

will also be outrightly defiant at times; but I find that often, we are dealing with our own unreasonable expectations for obedience. These expectations lead to biting and cutting punishment, instead of training our children in the way they should go by pointing them to Christ. We are tough on our kids because we can be—because we are the authority.

Iron fists chisel stony hearts, but graceful hands shape responsive hearts.

The book of James describes the avalanche of harm that can come when we yield to anger. In chapter 1, verses 19-20, James writes, "My dear brothers and sisters, take note of this: Everyone should be quick to listen, slow to speak and slow to become angry, because human anger does not produce the righteousness that God desires" (NIV). Often our anger leads to other sinful behaviors—impatience, rudeness, and harsh scolding, for example. I certainly don't respond well when someone treats me like that, so it's unreasonable to think that our kids will blossom under that kind of discipline either. With the Holy Spirit as our guide, we can transform our angry responses into loving ones that still hold our children to a godly standard of obedience while also demonstrating the Fruit of the Spirit toward them.

Let's tweak our parenting perspectives a bit.

Perhaps we need to view ourselves more like coaches. A

coach is an authority figure, too. A coach is part of a team. A coach doesn't expect the quality of an Olympic athlete or behavior on the first day of practice! An excellent coach sees a weakness and then assigns exercises to train her athletes intentionally. A coach does what I did on the track that day, though it was inconvenient for me: I slipped off my pumps, and ran beside my sweet, young student. When their athlete or musician or chess player fails, they don't bully them— they inspire, uplift, and give them wings to fly. Similarly, if we coach our kids through life, we become their cheerleaders too, offering them hope and confidence to become more like Christ.

As I parent my own children, I'm often reminded of that day on the track. Stacey stared straight down the final stretch of track toward the finish line as I ran beside her. She was almost there. The clock counted down a little too close for comfort, but just before her time was up, she stumbled over the chalk line, victorious. She had finished her race. Nearly ten years later, her mom emailed me to let me know that my decision to coach Stacey through her test that day was a turning point in her life. She realized that someone cared about her enough to run alongside her. Even if it was unconventional. Inconvenient. Unexpected. All the months of Bible study talk had little impact until I walked my talk—or ran it out right beside her in her P.E. class.

Yes, I could share parenting strategies with you to produce

obedient kids. And Wendy and I will do just that through each day of this book. But let's not focus on the end results and miss the opportunity to be refined alongside of them in the process. Let's embrace what it means to be *Mom as Coach*, patiently and lovingly training our kids toward the blessings of obedience.

LET'S PRAY:

"Dear God, You want all of Your children to be obedient. I know that when we obey You, we receive blessing and You are glorified. Father, I want to raise obedient children, but I also want to model obedience to You in my own life. Help me to see my kids through Your eyes and to be their enthusiastic coach, lovingly pointing them to Your standards with grace and truth, instead of anger. Replace my frustrations with mercy. Make me slow to anger! Help me to run alongside my children, championing them and loving them well, even when they disobey. May we all be more like You, Lord Jesus! Thank You for Your promises to help me become a godly mom! In Jesus' name, amen!"

Amber

CHAPTER 2: BACKTALK

....

When your children were young, you spoke words of life into their little beings. They cooed and you cooed back. You whispered blessings over them as they slept and told them "you are SO BIG" when they were so tiny. You had no intention of ever berating your babies. Even if you yourself were raised in a home full of heated arguments, explosive and loud, you never intended to pass that legacy down. And so you sang Scripture promises and memorized the golden rule. You were proactive in using tender words and shared the old adage, "If you don't have anything nice to say, don't say anything at all." And through it all you held great hope that your family would build each other up with lips dripping honey.

But before long, the honey grew rancid, and began tasting more like vinegar on your tongue. Within only a few short years, your toddler proved defiant, difficult, and demanding —as is their job at two. And you grew angry.

Since the start of those "terrible twos," a battle of words has raged between you and them; amongst siblings in backseats, and teenagers with backtalk. It started with simple "No, Mommy, no…" when changing diapers or serving peas, but before long, toddler lips pursed in negative words grew into loud yelling matches. And you're plain worn out from the warring and the shame. You want to retreat, but their constant bantering sets you off faster than anything else. It's your trigger —Kaboom! You bring out the big guns and end the skirmish with a few choice words, because your voice is the loudest.

The problem with this battle strategy is that when we attempt to discipline them with our own aggressive voices, we usurp the teachable moments. In other words, we steal the show with our own fit throwing. Think of it this way: When our children do wrong and we stay calm and controlled, they know that they've done wrong. They do! They know it down to their convicted little cores! There is power when we bend down, touch their shoulders, and look them in the eyes. "That wasn't a nice thing to say; can you try again?" **However, when we exchange angry words for angry words, nasty face for nasty face, slamming door for slamming door, and tear them down with our words because they tore us down with theirs, they will never feel remorse for their own actions.** We have hijacked that teachable moment. It's simple, but it's true!

I think this is what God means in Romans 2:4: "...God's kindness is meant to lead you to repentance." When we learn to parent like God parents us, out of a calm and stable sense of our own authority, our children have the holy opportunity to experience true repentance. They feel a healthy heartache over it and take ownership of their sin in the quiet spaces that we don't demolish with our loud and constant nagging. What a gift we give them when we stay in control. What a gift they forfeit when we blow up and talk back to their backtalk.

"Everyone enjoys a fitting reply; it is wonderful to say the right thing at the right time!" (Proverbs 15:23, NLT)

Yelling back at them when they yell is never the right thing at the right time. And so today we are slowing down in the quiet of these words to

FIGURE OUT WHAT YOU MEAN TO SAY BEFORE YOU SAY SOMETHING MEAN.

make a plan, that we might see the moments when they backtalk not as invitations to fight, but as opportunities to lead them kindly to repentance.

Before you react, consider the right response.

I have chosen, in moments void of conflict, a few phrases to use when their words are full of venom. Words like, "Son, I know that you don't want to fight with me. So when you are ready to talk, I am ready to listen." Similarly, "Honey, God didn't make me to fight you." Of course, this doesn't immediately quench their anger, so often I firmly tell them, "I need you to spend some time in your room so that you don't hurt our relationship with your words. Please stay there until I come to you. Then you will have a chance to tell me what's on your mind in a kind way."

Figure out what you mean to say before you say something mean.

Of course, because they're all amped up and ready for a fight, they often push through our gentle firewall with more back-talking reasons why they won't go to their room. Or they go and come immediately out with equally loud reasons why they are right and I'm an ogre! But I've made a commitment to The Lord, to myself, and to my family to not engage in the battle any more. So I walk them back to their room and repeat myself, "I will not fight you. I will talk with you in a little bit. Please wait for me."

In the quiet that follows, I remind myself that my children are allowed to make wrong choices; God calls this free will. It is not my job to strangle them into submission. I am responsible to navigate my own free choices, not control theirs. I can only hold captive my own tongue, leading by example, training them to do likewise, but I cannot badger them into repentance. Lord knows I've tried!

Which leads me to prayer. Only the Holy Spirit can meet my children in these quiet times, convicting their hearts, and in His kindness lead them to repentance and lasting change. Moms and dads, we have the awesome privilege to pray for our children. Pray for their hearts and their words.

I have received letters from exasperated moms, confessing to actually cussing at their young children and teenagers. They are shocked by their anger and the ease with which curse words and shaming blows flow out of their hearts. Parents are desperate for change—more desperate to change their own hearts than to change their children. From cover to cover in this book, we are taking a brief look at the things our children do wrong—that trigger our explosive responses— and then camping out on what God has to tell us about our own hearts.

Do we want to see our children obey? Of course! Are we prayerful that their words will be gentle and honoring? Absolutely. But we can't force peace to well up within them and spill out over their lips. That's not our job. We can only control our own tongues, as we yield to the power of the Holy Spirit at work in us.

LET'S PRAY:

"Dear Lord, slow me down. By the power of Your Holy Spirit, slow me down that I might consider my words

carefully. Empower me to build my loved ones up, even when they are attempting to tear the rest of us down in their own emotional angst. Let there be peace in our home, and let it begin with You at work in me. For it is no longer I who live, but You Who lives and speaks from within me. I want to respond as You would respond, rather than react in my flesh. Amen."

Wendy

CHAPTER 3: DISRESPECT

....

When my kids disrespect me, I can feel my back stiffen, my eyes narrow, and my breath catch. Our anger triggers will often alert us by the way our bodies physically respond. What comes across as disrespectful to me, however, may be perfectly acceptable in someone else's home. Regardless of what barometers we use to define respect, there are clear examples of reverence from a spiritual perspective. The website, GotQuestions.org, describes biblical respect like this:

"The word respect is a translation of the Greek word *timēsate*, meaning 'honor or value.' It literally means 'to place a great value or high price on something.' Interestingly, today we tend to place our values on our personal rights and the equality of man. However, biblical respect is far different, more about a perceived inequality in that we recognize that some things and some people are more important than we..."[1]

Biblical respect means valuing someone else more than we value ourselves. This thought is emphasized in Philippians 2:3: " Do nothing from selfish ambition or conceit, but in humility count others more significant than yourselves." This biblical picture of respect is a mature spiritual mindset, so we need to keep this in mind when our immature kids don't measure up to our expectations for respectful attitudes and actions. They need our kind instruction and humble example to grow in this area. And they certainly need our patience. Disrespect often feels like a personal attack. We think, "How dare they talk to me like that—I'm the *mother*!" In our mind's eye, we deserve respect simply because of our position. But immature kids don't revere positions for the sake of it. Instead, they often respect those that show them unconditional love and treat them as they would want to be treated. That sounds a lot like the Golden Rule, from Matthew 7:12:

> **WE CAN DEMAND RESPECT BECAUSE OF OUR RANK, OR WE CAN FOSTER RESPECT BECAUSE OF OUR RIGHTEOUSNESS.**

"So whatever you wish that others would do to you, do also to them, for this is the Law and the Prophets." Our ideas about respect begin to shift when we understand the level of maturity required to value others in this way.

There could be a myriad of reasons and ways our kids make us feel disrespected, but for our purposes, we need to first consider this question: What is the correct *biblical response* to our child when we feel they are disrespecting us?

As mothers, we can make it easier or harder for our children to value us. **We can demand respect because of our rank, or we can foster respect because of our righteousness.** Jesus faced false accusations, sarcasm, challenges to His authority, and outright abuse from people who mercilessly mocked Him:

> *"The men in charge of Jesus began poking fun at him, slapping him around. They put a blindfold on him and taunted, "Who hit you that time?" They were having a grand time with him." Luke 22:63-65, MSG*

And this…

> *"Herod was delighted when Jesus showed up. He had wanted for a long time to see him, he'd heard so much about him. He hoped to see him do something spectacular. He peppered him with questions. Jesus didn't answer—not one word. But the high priests and religion scholars were right there, saying their piece, strident and shrill in their accusations.*
>
> *Mightily offended, Herod turned on Jesus. His soldiers joined in, taunting and jeering. Then they dressed him up in an elaborate king costume and sent him back to Pilate. That day Herod and Pilate became thick as thieves. Always before they had kept their distance.*

Then Pilate called in the high priests, rulers, and the others and said, "You brought this man to me as a disturber of the peace. I examined him in front of all of you and found there was nothing to your charge. And neither did Herod, for he has sent him back here with a clean bill of health. It's clear that he's done nothing wrong, let alone anything deserving death. I'm going to warn him to watch his step and let him go."

At that, the crowd went wild: "Kill him! Give us Barabbas!" (Barabbas had been thrown in prison for starting a riot in the city and for murder.) Pilate still wanted to let Jesus go, and so spoke out again.

But they kept shouting back, "Crucify! Crucify him!"

He tried a third time. "But for what crime? I've found nothing in him deserving death. I'm going to warn him to watch his step and let him go."

But they kept at it, a shouting mob, demanding that he be crucified. And finally they shouted him down. Pilate caved in and gave them what they wanted. He released the man thrown in prison for rioting and murder, and gave them Jesus to do whatever they wanted." Luke 23: 8-25, MSG

And later, while on the cross:

"The soldiers also came up and poked fun at him, making a game of it. They toasted him with sour wine: "So you're King of the Jews! Save yourself!"

Printed over him was a sign: this is the king of the Jews."
Luke 23:36-38, MSG

So then, moms, what is Jesus' response to their incredible contempt for His authority and position as Jesus, Son of God?

"He was oppressed and treated harshly, yet he never said a word. He was led like a lamb to the slaughter. And as a sheep is silent before the shearers, he did not open his mouth." Isaiah 53:7, MSG

"Jesus prayed, "Father, forgive them; they don't know what they're doing." Luke 23:34-35, MSG

Talk about being disrespected, huh?

We live in a world where we are taught to nip things in the bud immediately, and in some ways there is a time and place for that. But we must examine how Jesus responds to disrespect. He loved. He forgave. He asked them questions to make them think—with simple Truth. And then He prayed, submitting Himself and His own reactions of His unjust trial to His Heavenly Father.

What about us? Do we bristle in anger or let our guards down when kids treat us disrespectfully?

How to act like Jesus when our children are disrespectful

1. Remain calm.

When Jesus' disciple cut off the ear in defense of Jesus in the Garden, Jesus rebuked him and restored the ear, healing the soldier who came to arrest Jesus. He kept His divine composure and modeled self-control to His disciples even in the face of unfair treatment and attack, even going so far as to right the wrong of another.

2. Speak the Truth in love.

With a compassionate and considerate attitude, we can say something like, "Son, your tone of voice comes across as unkind and I don't think you are showing me respect. If you would like to talk in a calm and normal voice about this issue, then you can come find me in the other room when you are ready to speak nicely so we can work this out."

Or:

"When you call me a name, you are saying words to tear me

down and that is sinful. God asks us to speak with grace and to build others up. I'm going to think about how I can help you with this issue and we can talk about it tomorrow. In the meantime, I would suggest you come up with at least one good idea yourself; otherwise, we will go with my plan instead." And then drop the matter, allowing them to feel the weight of responsibility for their wrongdoing. So many times, my sons have had time to think about their wrong behavior and have come to me hours later in tears to ask for forgiveness. Those teachable moments allowed time for the Holy Spirit to genuinely convict them and lead them to true repentance.

3. Pray!

Jesus prayed fervently over His burden in the Garden of Gethsemane and He emerged strengthened to face the treachery that lay before Him. If the disrespect is high in your home, OUT PRAY it! As Wendy pointed out yesterday, it's not our role to change the hearts of our kids. It's God's job to do that. We fight the battle for their hearts in prayer!

4. Forgive.

You can choose to forgive your child's disrespect even if they never ask for forgiveness. Jesus recognized that mankind didn't even fully grasp what they were doing in their impertinence. Often, our kids don't fully grasp the impact, either. Be patient with them. Part of forgiveness is yielding your desire to make someone pay for their offense. Forgiveness offers freedom to ourselves, as much as for the offender.

5. Just do the right thing.

Jesus yielded to doing the right thing—dying on the cross—even though it caused Him to suffer and there was no guarantee that the people He agonized for would change. He died anyway. We, too, can be long-suffering when we deal with people who seem they will never change: when we love them like Jesus does, it's very hard not to change with time under the power of loving-kindness. You can never go wrong by doing what is right!

6. Commit yourself to your Heavenly Father.

There comes a time when you do the right thing and you must leave the results up to God. If your kids don't ever become the respectful adults that God requires of them, it is not your burden to carry. That is between them and God. Commit yourself to the Lord and live out the Fruit of the Spirit in your own life, trusting God to transform the lives of your loved ones in His timing.

I don't need to be caught off guard when my kids don't show me the reverence I feel I deserve; I can use it as an opportunity to reflect on my own deference to Christ's authority over my life when I was immature and lost, and how He bent down to lovingly restore me anyway. **When my kids' disrespectful actions trigger my anger, I can turn reflective instead of reactive.** Those moments are opportunities for me to consider whether or not I value them enough to hold my tongue and treat them with the respect that they are not showing to me. I believe that when we parent our children with the same loving-kindness that Jesus demonstrates towards us, in time, they, too, will value and esteem us.

Should we teach our kids to respect us? Absolutely.

WHEN MY KIDS' DISRESPECTFUL ACTIONS TRIGGER MY ANGER, I CAN TURN REFLECTIVE INSTEAD OF REACTIVE.

Will it go well for them if they honor their father and mother? Indeed. But the process of parenting inconsiderate sons and daughters begins with our own humility—a bearing-our-own-cross kind of humility that yields our rights to the way we want to be treated in exchange for grace.

LET'S PRAY:

"Lord Jesus, Thank You for enduring the pain and blatant disrespect of the cross for me. You humbled Yourself in the face of outright hatred, loving Your enemies. Thank You for Your example to me as a mother! It's Your blood that washes away my sinful pride. I want to respond with gentle words that allow Your Holy Spirit to convict my children. Lord, help me to teach my kids how to respect me without becoming angry. Replace my hurt feelings with patience and understanding. I love You, Lord, for loving me, even when I was unlovely. May my children also know the depth of Your love for them, because they see the same love modeled in me. In Jesus' name, amen!"

Amber

CHAPTER 4: STRONG-WILLED CHILDREN

My first-born was three years old, his little brother was only one, and my belly was full of a third-born son. I arrived early to church that autumn morning, got my boys settled into their classes, then waddled to the gym for my weekly MOPS group. After sampling three different egg dishes and every muffin, quick bread, bagel, and donut on the potluck table, I found my friends and settled into good kid-free conversation.

The gals were all talking about their challenging mornings with their challenging children, excited that our guest that day would be speaking on raising strong-willed kids. I was interested too, because my firstborn seemed hard-wired strong; argumentative, oppositional, and always asking for more or different. Truth be told, I was eager to learn tools that would help me *fix him.*

When the speaker took the podium that morning, she began by sharing story after story of how her daughter had pushed boundaries, not listened, thrown tantrums, and fought tirelessly for her own way...from the time she was a toddler. This child was such a handful from the very beginning that her mom decided to make her an only child. Raising this one little power-packed person took everything she had.

I leaned forward to glean any and all hard-earned parenting wisdom she had to share with us that morning...only she didn't follow up with any practical advice about what we could do to change our children. Not a lick of help! What she did do, however, was tell us more stories—stories about what a strong-willed little boy or girl can look like on the other side of childhood.

Her daughter was finishing up her undergraduate work at an impressive private college. Extremely active in an on-campus Christian ministry, she was passionate about sharing her faith in Christ every chance she got. That meant summer internships and short-term mission trips, hosting Bible studies for non-Christians in her college dorm room, and defending her faith in secular classes. She was a beautiful girl with a wild mane of hair, and her mother spoke of her daughter's commitment to remain sexually pure until marriage.

That mother's main point became very clear before she brought it all together at the end: Strong-willed children grow up into strong-willed adults! I know it's miserably hard when they're throwing fits over a bag of goldfish at the grocery store, but one day that tenacity is going to serve them well when they face peer pressure and worldly temptations. Because of what we are doing right now, "training them up in the way they will go, " they will be the last to depart from the righteous path!

> # STRONG-WILLED CHILDREN WERE DESIGNED TO CLING TENACIOUSLY TO THE STRONGEST WILL OF ALL...THE WILL OF GOD.

It is my prayer that one day we, too, will see their stick-to-it-iveness as a blessing, when we look at it from the backside of these challenging years. God made our children strong-willed, so that once they put their faith in Him and submit to His will, they will not be detoured. Those iron wills will not fail. **Strong-willed children were designed to cling tenaciously to the strongest will of all...the will of God.**

Unattended, a strong-willed child can grow up into an unruly, aggressive, argumentative personality that no one wants to be around. They lose their friends and their jobs and even their marriages, because they roll like a steam engine over everyone and everything in their path. However, with the consistent and long-suffering care of a mother, these strong-willed kids grow up to be world changers!

Praise God!

Still, despite all that good head knowledge, the reality can be hard. When your children flex their strong-will muscles all day long, I know that you feel worn out and worked over; but let me encourage you to choose your words carefully. It's hard to do when you're reacting impulsively to their strong and wrong behavior, but it is paramount. Parents of strong-willed children must choose words that build up their God-design, not tear it down with blame and shame. God didn't make a mistake when He made them tenacious. You honor God when you honor your child's hardwiring, even if their personality rubs you wrong. I often tell my strong-willed kids, "God did a good job when He made you. Now let's figure out how He would have you to behave in this moment."

When they were toddlers, I'd say it plainly, "Sweetheart, you are throwing a very big fit right now. Can you use that same passion to do what I'm asking you right now? Because I love how big your heart is. I love how much you feel! But you have to master all those emotions." Perhaps you have an older child who is pushing for their independence, muscling through the family like a bull in the china shop of your home. "Honey, you are pushing me right now. You are very determined and that's a good character trait if you can control yourself! You must use your strength rightly, or you will have a hard time with friendships and work relationships. You get to practice this stuff on me first."

And isn't that the truth? God put us together with these children that they might learn how to behave in relationships with others. We are the safe place where they get to learn how to fit their God-design appropriately into life beyond our home. When we constantly criticize and correct, we are *not* that safe place. They need to feel accepted just as they are, even if their behavior is unacceptable.

Let us not undo them in our attempts to redo them better, but let us partner with the One who made them for His glory – strong-willed, tenacious, and fierce!

I have one more point to share about my own journey raising strong-willed children. I think that I would have been quite proud of myself if everything had been easy—had I been given compliant children. I am naturally a nurturer, so full of love towards my kiddos; I am creative in teaching them and tucking them in and leading them in the study of God's Word. And yet they are challenging at every turn. Though I've often felt like a failure, I'm starting to see my quiver of strong-willed arrows as a blessing. Because when all is said and done, and the beauty of His plan for their lives bears fruit, I won't be able to take any credit myself. I think I would have been proud for the way they turned out if it had been easier. But as it is…they belong to Him. From conception to completion, all His. And there's nothing left for me to do, but trust Him!

LET'S PRAY:

"Dear Lord, I need your wisdom to point my strong-willed children to You each and every day. Show me how to lead them so that I don't shame them in their unique design. I want to build them up, not tear them down. I want to honor their design, and in so doing honor You, their Creator. I choose today to trust You, and Your plan for their lives. They are fearfully and wonderfully made. You did a good job when You wove their will tight like steel. Show them how to use that strength appropriately, for Your glory! I ask this all in Jesus' name. Amen."

Wendy

CHAPTER 5: ANGRY KIDS

....

I'm not sure that there is anything more disheartening to the heart of a mom than realizing that she has an angry child—a son or daughter who seems to move about with a dark cloud hovering over them, who flies off the handle at the slightest request, who lashes out at his or her siblings or classmates.

The issue of anger in our children is as multi-faceted as all the jewels on Rodeo Drive in Beverly Hills. As moms who struggle with anger, we often fear that we are modeling this hotheaded behavior and that our kids are picking up on it. We may not like to hear it, but we have to begin with examining *ourselves* to help our kids overcome anger.

The biblical command is clear: "Fathers, do not provoke your children to anger, but bring them up in the discipline and instruction of the Lord." (Ephesians 6:4) This verse isn't just for fathers, is it? Moms shouldn't provoke children to anger, either. The *MacArthur New Testament Commentary on Ephesians*, describes provocation like this:

"To 'provoke...to anger' suggests a repeated, ongoing pattern of treatment that gradually builds up a deep–seated anger and resentment that boils over in outward hostility."[2]

So how do we respond to the anger in the lives of our children? First, we stop provoking them. Here's a list of just a few ways we can exasperate our kids and create an anger problem for them. Prayerfully read through this list and honestly reflect whether or not you have contributed to your child's anger problem:

- Unreasonable expectations.

- Inconsistent standards among siblings.

- Favoritism.

- Punishing them in anger.

- Scolding or lecturing.

- Physical or verbal abuse.

- Discouragement or not praising them enough.

- Conflicts in our marriage.

- Our own inability to ask for forgiveness.

- Not listening to them or hearing them out in a reasonable manner.

- Restricting them too much or controlling their every move.

- Failing to keep our promises.

- Belittling them.

- Constant fault-finding.

- Overprotecting.

- Taking our anger with someone or something else out on our kids.

I know this list is convicting, but we honestly can't address our children's anger unless we first take ownership for our part. THAT is the biblical response to our child's anger! We must first discipline ourselves, before we consider training or teaching our children.

No one respects a hypocrite:

> *"Why do you see the speck that is in your brother's eye, but do not notice the log that is in your own eye? 42 How can you say to your brother, 'Brother, let me take out the speck that is in your eye,' when you yourself do not see the log that is in your own eye? You hypocrite, first take the log out of your own eye, and then you will see clearly to take out the speck that is in your brother's eye." (Luke 6:41-42)*

Hypocrisy is holding others to a standard that we do not hold to ourselves.

Here are a few questions to ask ourselves to see if we have set a bar for our sons and daughters that we do not live up to in our own lives as moms, thus provoking them to anger:

- Is my goal in every word and deed to help my kids become Christ-like? Or am I trying to "fix" them?

- Am I trying to correct my kids by taking the splinter out of their eyes while missing the log in my own?

- Am I growing in gentleness as a wife and mom?

- Do I feel that I must correct every error on my children's part, or do I often cover their sin with my love?

- Am I forgetting the developmental age of my kids (and thus expecting too much from them)?

- When was the last time I asked them questions to resolve an issue instead of simply lecturing them?

- Do my kids feel that they have a voice? (There's a thought! Man, we could just camp out there for a whole chapter!)

- Do I believe that I can get discernment from the Holy Spirit for every aspect of my parenting, and am I praying for that on a daily basis?

Much of the growth in our own spiritual walk is a result of being refined by motherhood. We certainly do not want to raise angry children, but first we must extinguish whatever embers we have stoked with our own words and shortcomings in our parenting.

The great news is that God longs to help us and He always answers the righteous prayers of His children who long to do the right thing! Don't be discouraged by any conviction that the Lord may be laying on your heart! Allow holy conviction to catapult you towards spiritual growth.

Moms don't need to be perfect, but we must yield to being perfected in Christ!

Ensuring our kids feel safe, encouraged, justly treated, and unconditionally loved goes a long way to dissolve their own anger issues. In some cases, it may take a significant amount of time to change the culture of your angry home, but it can be done, one mom and one moment—at a time. Shift your focus from trying to "fix" their tempers and persevere through prayer. Ask the Lord to search your heart and reveal to you His wisdom to become a more gentle and Christ-centered mom, so that neither you nor your children are displaying sinful anger.

MOMS DON'T NEED TO BE PERFECT, BUT WE MUST YIELD TO BEING PERFECTED IN CHRIST!

LET'S PRAY:

"Father, I don't want my child to be angry because of anything I have done. Reveal to me the ways that I may be provoking my child to anger and forgive me. Help me to feel Your love for me, even when I mess up, and allow me to love and teach my kids in a godly way. Soften the heart of my child, and help me to be patient as You transform my heart and theirs. Thank You for convicting me, but not condemning me! Thank You for promising to give me wisdom to reach my angry child. In Jesus' name, amen!"

Amber

CHAPTER 6: WHINING AND COMPLAINING

There is one word...no, it's more like a sound...that has the power to stop a toddler's whining cries faster than any other. It is the glorious and effective "Uh-oh." Especially useful for a mother, like me, who tends to lecture every little wrong my children commit, "Uh-oh" lets them know that you know they've made a poor choice. It's also the sound that naturally comes out of their own mouths when they realize they've made a mistake, or simply tripped and fallen down.

Uh-oh.

"Uh-oh" reminds us that mistakes happen. And it sounds so much nicer and more gracious than, "How many times have I told you not to..."

My youngest child had a new teacher at his swim class this morning. I heard Ms. Rebecca's sweet voice sing "Uh-oh" a few times during their 20-minute lesson. It effectively pulled his focus back and at the same time reminded me what a splendid tool I often forsake in lieu of nagging and harsh correction.

Uh-oh.

I've heard that we need to say 10 encouraging things to our children for every one correction. For goodness' sake! I'm a naturally encouraging person, but I don't think I can fit that much positive affirmation in while correcting three young boys all day long! And then this morning it occurred to me that I don't need to fit more encouragement in (there is plenty in our home)—what I need to do is trash a good deal of the criticism. Gently acknowledging wrong behavior, reminding them that mistakes happen with a genuine "Uh-oh," and helping them remember the way our family treats one another doesn't have to be done with a stern voice, a disapproving face, or even criticism.

Another simple tactic is to merely say, "I'm sorry, sweetheart, I don't understand what you're saying. Can you use your big boy voice?" How much nicer is that than a harsh, "Stop your complaining... all you ever do is whine and pitch fits!"

Uh-oh.

Our heart's desire, both yours and mine, is to speak life into the hearts of our children. But their incessant whining and complaining can wear us down and pull the hammer to our trigger back faster than the time it takes to breathe the word "Uh-oh." So today, we're asking ourselves, what's the biblical response to their complaining hearts instead of flipping out and joining them in the grumbling?

Three things to consider when your children start to complain:

1. Behave right when they behave wrong. It is the most ridiculous thing in the world that we correct our children with the same wrong behavior we're telling them not to do. **They whine and complain, so we whine and complain about their whining and complaining, thinking this will make them stop whining and complaining.**

Do you ever feel like you meet them in their wrong behavior, rather than minister to them from a place of serene authority? I know that I do this sometimes. The key is remembering who the adult is. Their job is to be children. Our job is to be adults: Teaching them how to grow up and out of their childishness into maturity. It's a simple equation that shouldn't take us by surprise. They are children, and we are their parents. **Whining is not a sin, it's merely a sign: a sign that they still have a few things to learn**—and we still have

> WHINING IS NOT A SIN, IT'S MERELY A SIGN: A SIGN THAT THEY STILL HAVE A FEW THINGS TO LEARN.

things to model well. "Uh-oh, Honey, let's try that again."

This is hardest, of course, when your children aren't toddlers anymore. Though you are ready for them to mature in this regard, sometimes the fruit is slow-growing. Therefore, we must press on in our own contentment despite the challenges.

2. Use God's Word like a scalpel, not a hammer. Christian moms are especially good at wielding God's Word like a hammer pounding on the head of a nail. We quote Philippians 2:14-15, at them all day long, each time they whine: "Do everything without grumbling or arguing, so that you may become blameless and pure children of God..." (NIV). But all they hear from us is the same nag-nagging.

Do you use Scripture when you're frustrated and angry? God's Word was never intended to be a hammer in the hand of an angry mom, but a surgeon's scalpel used in tandem with the Holy Spirit's guidance. When we meet our children, in the height of their fit-throwing tantrums, with Bible verses... we wield the sword of truth inappropriately. It's like attempting surgery before the patient is under anesthesia, before the surgeon has properly scrubbed up.

We don't plant seeds in hard soil, either. We toil it first, conditioning the earth with the proper tools, and at just the right time we place the seeds carefully and lovingly into the ground. So it is with little hearts in need of Scripture truth.

I'm not saying that we shouldn't use Scriptures to train them up in the ways they are to go; I'm just saying that we shouldn't use them to shame our kids in the middle of the battle. Let them calm down first, as you take a few moments to calm down, too. And let the Holy Spirit do His own convicting work. Then, once their hearts are soft, go in and plant those perfect seeds.

> *"As the rain and the snow come down from heaven, and do not return to it without watering the earth and making it bud and flourish, so that it yields seed for the sower and bread for the eater, so is my word that goes out from my mouth: It will not return to me empty, but will accomplish what I desire and achieve the purpose for which I sent it." Isaiah 55:10-11, NIV*

3. Act like a child of God! One of the overarching themes of this whole book is the need take our frazzled focused off of our children's behavior, and fix our eyes firmly on our own hearts. Is it possible, if you're being totally honest, that you have the same toddler tendencies that your children have? Do you huff and puff and walk through the room with heavy, discontented footsteps? Do your words tear down and tease out arguments, or do they build up and speak life to your family members? And have you applied Philippians 2:14-15 to your own life, before preaching at your own children?

"Do everything without grumbling or arguing, so that you may become blameless and pure children of God..."

I once heard a pastor deliver these words to His congregation in the most marvelous manner. He told us that the best way to understand the word "become" in the verses above is to think of it as becoming, or acting like, the child of God that you already are because of your faith in Christ. When you understand that you are already blameless and pure because of what Christ did for you upon that cross, then *becoming* His children really means *behaving* like it.

Do everything without grumbling, complaining or arguing, so that you may behave like the blameless and pure child of God that you already are! Ladies, we want this from our children, but God wants this for us. We have already been made holy through faith in Christ. Now it's time we act like it. Of course, this takes the spiritual fruit of self-control; minding our tongues and behaving rightly. But the fruit in our lives becomes a generational gift! They learn from us as we hold every thought captive, before it leaks in negative ways out over our lips and into our homes.

Let us do these mothering years well, without complaining or arguing, without whining or shaming, that we might act like the blameless and pure children of God we already are!

LET'S PRAY:

"Dear Lord, I want to behave like I'm Your child. I want to look like You, Abba. Even when the rest of the world grumbles and complains, I want Your praise to be forever on my lips. Help me to be content in every and all circumstances, Lord, that I might model this life, as a true child of God, for my own children. With You this is possible, Amen."

Wendy

CHAPTER 7: SIBLING RIVALRY

For Christmas one year, our boys received a large bouncy house from Grandma and Grandpa. We figured that it would burn all that extra energy off in a safe environment; what we didn't figure is how much arguing it would foster, too. My three boys battled it out over who was making up the games to play in the bouncy house, whether or not that knee to the stomach was intentional or an accident, and who had to be in charge of putting it away.

Have you ever felt like your kids' sibling rivalry is a sure sign that you are not a good parent?

I sure did.

But I have good news for you! Sibling rivalry is human nature. I don't know a family on earth that hasn't struggled with this issue. Arguing between our children is not always an indicator that we are bad parents! Unfortunately, I used to match the arguing between my kids with equal frustration, volume, and discouragement. Not exactly a godly response. I needed to reframe the way I thought about sibling rivalries to view them as *opportunities*.

TRIGGERS=OPPORTUNITIES if we choose to handle them that way.

So often, we think of triggers as a bother. A problem. Something to nip in the bud. Life will present us with many situations that will trigger us to react in sinful anger. If we can reorient our thinking about these triggers to see them as opportunities, we can be spiritually victorious. Every trigger is an opportunity in one way or another. Here's what I mean regarding sibling rivalry:

Sibling rivalry is an opportunity for two good things to happen:

1. My boys learn how to identify their feelings, communicate well, and problem solve.

And,

2. I learn to respond biblically and train my kids in righteousness.

In our home, we set the standard by first creating a short list of family values—like making our home a place of peace by becoming peacemakers. We talk this Biblical idea over with our kids, giving examples of how we can all be agents for peace in our home. If sibling rivalry is rampant, one of the best biblical responses we can give our kids is to memorize a passage from the Bible that relates to the issue. This section from Romans 12:17-20 is one of my favorites when harmony is being overshadowed by discord:

> *"Do not repay anyone evil for evil. Be careful to do what is right in the eyes of everyone. If it is possible, as far as it depends on you, live at peace with everyone. Do not take revenge, my dear friends, but leave room for God's wrath, for it is written: "It is mine to avenge; I will repay," says the Lord. On the contrary:*
> *'If your enemy is hungry, feed him;*
> *if he is thirsty, give him something to drink.*
> *In doing this, you will heap burning coals on his head.'" (NIV)*

This verse is foundational to dealing with all kinds of fighting and arguing. Take the time to talk through it little by little over the course of a few weeks. Ask your kids questions about what they think it means and how they can apply it to an example in their own lives. Tease out scenarios from your own day and how you can model this to your kids. Speak in a loving and positive tone whenever you approach Scripture, not in a way that communicates condemnation or punishment. Remember, we want our kids to see the Word of God as the path to life, offering hope through Scripture, not a tool to shame them!

Once that groundwork has been laid as a standard for

behavior in our home, the proof is in the pudding.

Try following these basic steps:

1. Separate them or intervene to calm them down.

This way, you can get to the real heart of the matter. It might mean asking them to go to different rooms for a 5-minute break while everyone cools down or dries their tears. It also gives you a moment to pray for wisdom!

2. Listen and investigate.

Too many times I have thought the wrong child was the instigator when he wasn't, so be sure to get the full picture. Sometimes, the best response from us is to ignore more minor offenses and simply tell our kids that we believe they can work it out themselves and to take it outside. Boost their confidence in their ability to take responsibility to handle conflicts. We wouldn't allow situations of extreme bullying or physical danger or harm to continue without our intervention; but there are lots of situations that we would do well to ignore, allowing our kids to practice healthy conflict resolution—especially if we are practicing this with them in times of peace and calm as part of our regular goal to parent well. When they are young, the stakes are low; this is the best time to let them begin to take ownership for their more trivial problems. Practice being a listener and a guide, instead of a fixer.

3. Ask questions about their feelings.

When arguments happen, it's usually because one or the other is feeling powerless. They aren't mature enough to communicate their feelings. When I say, "Quinn, is this making you feel sad because you were playing with that toy and your brother grabbed it away from you without asking?" it gives him a voice to explain his frustration, instead of crying or hitting his little brother. It also makes him feel heard and validated, giving him back some sense of security.

Then I can ask the other sibling, "How do you think you would feel if you were playing with a toy and Quinn took it from you?" Inquiring in a matter-of-fact way gives us an opportunity to train our kids in Christ-like behavior. When they consider the "Golden Rule" of treating one another as they would want to be treated themselves, that truth sinks in much more effectively than if we rush in, punish both kids, and move on to dinner preparations or ironing the laundry.

4. Use natural consequences and show empathy.

Sometimes, I simply let the natural consequences or even "projected consequences" do all the work. In the scenario we have been discussing, I say something like, "I guess that means you don't really want to play with Oakley anymore today, huh, Quinn?"

"Boy, Oakley, I'm so sad that you made that wrong choice. You could have had such a fun time with your brother, but it looks like you won't get to play with him today. What a bummer. I'm sure he still loves you, but you should probably give him some space now."

When we offer our kids all the solutions, we rob them of opportunities to mature.

I don't need to try and "fix" every conflict for my boys. Allowing them to feel the weight and loss that their wrong choices bring into their lives is the best teaching tool because it puts ownership on THEM. My role is to show sincere empathy and concern for them, mingled with confidence that they will choose a better path next time!

5. Forgive and move on.

Sibling rivalry is an occasion to teach what forgiveness looks like—giving up our need or desire for revenge. It also gives us the chance to model the concept that love does not keep a record of wrongs. What a gift it would be to ingrain that truth in the hearts of our children now, so that in future relationships, they don't let themselves become embittered and hardened by other's failures or sin. That means that we as moms need to forgive our kids too—and then commit to not bringing it up again or feeling resentful towards our children. For us, this becomes a refining moment if we let it.

You don't need a bouncy house to know that sibling rivalry can spring up at any moment and for a myriad of reasons. The key is that we must continue to model a calm and gentle approach so that we don't add fuel to the flame. Proverbs 15:18 warns us that "A hot-tempered man stirs up strife,

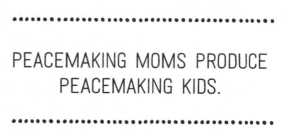

PEACEMAKING MOMS PRODUCE PEACEMAKING KIDS.

but he who is slow to anger quiets contention." We can equip our kids with tools to use their words and teach them to consider one another's feelings. **Peacemaking moms produce peacemaking kids.**

When conflicts erupt, don't become discouraged as if their arguing is a benchmark for your mothering. Give it time. Most of us would like our kids' quarrels and arguments to end yesterday, but the intricacy of learning to relate to others is no quick endeavor. 1 Corinthians 13:11 reminds us, "When I was a child, I spoke like a child, I thought like a child, I reasoned like a child. When I became a man, I gave up childish ways." Simply take advantage of that opportunity to cultivate peace amongst siblings one squabble at a time, and the harvest will come in the form of loving relationships when they are grown.

LET'S PRAY:

"Heavenly Father, It unnerves me when my kids fight with one another, and it often makes me feel like a failure. I want them to get along, but I know that takes time and maturity. Lord, I need Your guidance to know what to do in these situations. Give me the words to say and the creative ideas to help my children become peacemakers. Thank You, Jesus, for promoting peace in our hearts through the Holy Spirit. Help us to put one another's needs before our own. Make our home a place of harmony and kindness. In Jesus' name, amen!"

Amber

CHAPTER 8: IGNORING INSTRUCTION

Last night, I set the table and made a lovely dinner. Everything was ready, so I called them to the dining room. "Sweetheart...kiddos...dinner's on the table." It was all rather June Cleaver—only I was wearing yoga pants and a stretched out tank rather than a tweed pencil skirt and a starched white blouse. Still, dinner smelled fantastic, my heart was soft and my words were kind—and I was sure everyone was going to love my culinary offering to the family.

Except no one came. No one. Not my husband, who was finishing an expense report for work, not my older boy playing his guitar, nor the two younger children, who were in their rooms, but all within ear shot.

Would this have set you off? Does their "selective hearing" make you feel powerless, disrespected, and insignificant? Maybe you feel anger wash over you fierce and fast at the mere thought of being ignored...again. But others of us don't get mad...we get sad. That's my tendency, anyway.

So I walked slowly to my husband's office and leaned in, "I've made a nice dinner and it's hot on the table, would you please join us?" Then I walked to the hallway where I could look into each of the boys' rooms. "Boys, I called you to the table for dinner, please wash up and come now."

This is how it starts for me, every time. Calm and kind. But eventually, when only one male person comes to the table after another gentle reminder, **my feelings of powerlessness erupt into an unhealthy display of power.** That's when sad turns to mad.

And I get mad at them for making me mad, for taking my gentle heart and abusing it so! My intentions were good, my words were joy-filled, my plan was love, and my offering generous. But when I realized, in no uncertain terms, that no one was listening to me...I broke down.

Maybe you feel powerless sometimes, too, both in your mothering and your marriage, and maybe at work as well. It can be so difficult to stay centered and serene when we feel we must FIGHT TO BE HEARD. However, what would God prefer for us? To fight this way, or to learn new skills that look more like Jesus? I would rather learn new Christ-like tools for healthy and effective communication than give into loud and shaming communication that won't actually help anyone to respond differently the next day.

Yelling doesn't change behavior long-term. But you already know that. Oh, it might get them to the table in the moment, but they won't remember when your gentle voice bids them come the next day. Have you ever wondered about that? Why does your yelling work in a heated moment, but the next time you speak in a soft, hallowed tone, it's back to being ignored? It's simple: **The power of a loud voice isn't real power**—what we need is to find real power in healthy, clear communication.

What we need are new skills.

And so this morning at the breakfast table, after working to round everyone up again, I found a gentle moment and told everyone that I needed their help (my husband included). "Hey, you guys, I enjoy making meals for our family; however, it hurts my feelings when you ignore me. When you ask me to come see what you're drawing or ask me to bring you an iced tea when you're mowing the yard, I wipe my hands off and come to you. But when I work to serve you dinner, and ask you all to come, I am most often flat-out ignored. This doesn't make any sense to me. Eventually, I get mad and you come, but mostly I'm just sad that you don't respect me and the ways I serve and care for you. I need this to change. And you need this to change, too, because the way you treat me will be the way you grow to treat other women. Does that make sense?"

The lesson went seemingly deep, and they all apologized.

That night I reminded them again. I got down on their level

and looked them in the eyes before dinnertime: "Guys, dinner is almost ready. Please tell me that you remember our talk at the table this morning and that you will come quickly and with a thankful heart when I call you in five minutes." Likewise, I went to my husband, working on his car out in the garage. "Dinner is going to be ready in five minutes. I really need you to help me teach the boys to come when they are called. Will you be able to join us in five minutes?"

Of course, dinner is only my example. However, this can go all day long, being ignored and feeling powerless—sad until you're just plain MAD! But right now, in your calm and collected place, consider those times you feel most unappreciated and unheard. **The times you feel most powerless are likely the times you explode in a fresh display of inappropriate power.** Grappling for control. Maybe it's when you ask for help cleaning up and no one responds; or when you call kids to the car, grabbing lunch boxes and heading out the door, hollering for them to follow.

In this safe place, right now, void of conflict, consider

THE TIMES YOU FEEL MOST POWERLESS ARE LIKELY THE TIMES YOU EXPLODE IN A FRESH DISPLAY OF INAPPROPRIATE POWER.

how you might find real power in clear communication. If there are family dynamics that aren't working, and leave you feeling undervalued and invisible, then you need a plan. **Yelling isn't doing any good—there is no power for you there.**

Learning to communicate with my loved ones has been a very practical resource to help me climb out of this pit of powerlessness: Speaking words that communicate clear expectations and consequences; expressing my feelings in appropriate ways at appropriate times; teaching my children that if they learn to listen to and honor me, the rest of their relationships for the rest of their lives will go better. Yes, learning to communicate has been an effective tool that holds real power in my mothering life.

"Now God has not only raised the Lord, but will also raise us up through His power." (1 Corinthians 6:14, NASB)

That said, communication is not the source of all power. Good communication is a godly tool, but the real power behind all we do and say is found entirely in Christ alone. Abide in Him, that you might bear the fruit of His peaceful, purposeful, and powerful presence among your precious people.

LET'S PRAY:

"Being ignored wears me out, Lord. But You know the feeling, don't You? Heavenly Father, I am sorry for all of the times that I ignored Your voice and chose my own way. Please help me to be more like You in the way I respond to my own kids—long-suffering and full of grace, morning by morning. And also, Father, speak into my heart and give me new parenting tools, that I might learn how to communicate more effectively with my loved ones. You are a kind God, and want the best for us all, so teach me. Amen."

Wendy

CHAPTER 9: LYING AND DECEIT

"Quinn, did you throw your trash out the bathroom window instead of putting it in the can?" I asked my 5-year-old.

"No, mooooommmm!" he protested with an incredulous look on his face. I had taken him into his bedroom where we sat on his bed for what I call a "Mercy Seat Talk," a time where my kids can decompress and we can talk through their behavior with a spirit of love and mercy.

I had seen a pile of trash collecting suspiciously outside the bathroom window. Quinn is my inquisitive one whose passion is to be a scientist when he grows up. I figured he was being curious and had some scientific reason for doing this, but I could never catch him in the act.

I couldn't be certain if he was lying to me or not, but I had two choices, regardless.

One option was that I could react in anger and frustration, write him off as a liar and untrustworthy, and possibly miss an opportunity to discover what was going on in his heart so that I could steer him back to a path of righteousness. The other option was to confront him lovingly and truthfully.

I chose the latter option.

In a calm and sincere tone of voice, I said:

"Honey, I'm not sure if I believe you. I don't think you are trying to be naughty in this situation, and my goal isn't to punish you. You know what really matters to me? That you tell me the truth. That's the most important thing to me."

His posture relaxed. He dropped his gaze. And then he told me the truth. "Okay, Mommy. I did throw all the trash out the window. I was doing an experiment and I wanted to see what would happen to the trash after a few days. I'm sorry."

Quinn felt that he could eventually be honest with me because we have already established a relationship that is safe for him to come to me with the truth. He knows that I am not a mom who doles out punishment at the drop of a dime, and that if there is a consequence, he has a voice in the matter and will be able to take ownership for his choices. He knows I'm not a mom who is going to yell at him, fly off the handle, or become unreasonable in my anger. He knows that I want what is best for him and that my goal in parenting is not to hurt him, *but to help him.*

Here's what happened next:

"Sweetheart," I said. "Thank you for telling me the truth. That is what means the most to me. I know that was hard, but I'm proud of you for being honest. Even though you were simply trying to do an experiment, you did something that was wrong. We put trash in the trash can, only. And Jesus never wants us to lie to anyone. The Bible says that lying is an 'abomination' to God. He hates lying! So, you need to make this right. What do you think you can do to make this situation better and build trust with me again?"

I let him have some time to think about this. Sometimes, I tell him we can talk about our ideas later that day and then I drop it. But Quinn knew just what to do this time:

"Mommy" he said excitedly. "I'm going to go right now and clean up all the trash! And then I'll go around and pick up extra trash in the yard, too! I'll ask permission to do an experiment next time, Mom."

ONLY WHEN WE CREATE A SAFE ENVIRONMENT FOR HONESTY CAN WE HELP OUR KIDS BECOME TRUTH-TELLERS.

Off he went, happily willing to make the situation right. The boy literally skipped away. He didn't cry and get angry with me as if I had punished him in some unrelated way, like taking away his Legos. He took responsibility and ownership for his choices, and we kept our relationship intact, too. **If I had punished him after he was honest with me, he would quickly learn that it doesn't pay to be honest, and he would probably become an even better liar next time.** Avoiding pain would be the name of his game. Instead, this became a time for me to reach his heart and point him to Christ. He got the point, understood the heart issue, and took responsibility by thinking through how he could make it right. All of these are ways I want to reach my child's heart for lasting change and for building Godly character.

Only when we create a safe environment for honesty can we help our kids become truth-tellers.

This brings me to one more sensitive point about chronic liars in our homes. I want to very carefully and tenderly bring up one aspect of this issue for you to consider. It may not apply to everyone reading this book, but I hope you will prayerfully consider what I'm about to say. Imagine this:

Let's say you are a young kid. Immature. You have a mom who is angry. Maybe a dad, too. They yell at you. They don't seem to take the log in their eye seriously, but take every opportunity to punish you for your sin.

Mom and Dad get exasperated with you. Tell you they don't

ever believe you. Wear you down with their words. Or maybe they just frown all the time and you feel like you are a burden to them.

And in general, because you have an angry mom, you get in trouble a lot. Sometimes just because you are immature and don't know any better.

So to avoid punishment, or yelling, or consequences, you start lying.

To avoid the pain.

To avoid hearing the anger and yelling...again.

You *become* a LIAR.

And the cycle continues.

You don't feel unconditionally loved. Because you are a child, you don't know how to navigate this home-life filled with angst and volatile emotions. There are no clear expectations, so you move through daily life on edge.

You don't even know what is okay and not okay because your mom and dad seem to get angry over anything. So you lie over little things and big things with no rhyme or reason —just to try to protect yourself from whatever unpredictable punishment may be coming down the pike for you.

Mom, would you be willing to prayerfully consider what kind of people you are making your kids into because you don't deal with your own sin first?

Because we CAN embitter and discourage them:

> *"Fathers, do not embitter your children, or they will become discouraged." (Colossians 3:21, NIV)*

We CAN exasperate them:

> *"Fathers, do not exasperate your children; instead, bring them up in the training and instruction of the Lord." (Ephesians 6:4, NIV)*

When our kids lie, the Biblical response for us as moms is to confront them with the truth in love and to examine how we may be contributing to shaping them into liars. I know that I am prone to share my struggles and seek change with people who love me and who I know will not judge me harshly or heap punishment on my head. In the same way, it's God's loving-kindness that draws us to repentance. Our kids need that too.

Ultimately, it's the Word of God that is active, so when we plant Truth in our hearts and in the hearts of our children, we begin to see lasting change. If lying is an issue in your home, consider these verses for memorization:

"There are six things that the Lord hates, seven that are an abomination to him: haughty eyes, a lying tongue, and hands that shed innocent blood, a heart that devises wicked plans, feet that make haste to run to evil, a false witness who breathes out lies, and one who sows discord among brothers." (Proverbs 6:16-19)

"Whoever desires to love life and see good days, let him keep his tongue from evil and his lips from speaking deceit." (1 Peter 3:10)

"Do not lie to one another, seeing that you have put off the old self with its practices and have put on the new self, which is being renewed in knowledge after the image of its creator." (Colossians 3:9-10)

Quinn hasn't lied to me since that incident. He learned integrity that day. Not just because he learned to tell the truth, but because he saw in his mom a woman of her word who wouldn't just be fair: she would untangle his fragile web of lies with grace and offer him something better than his false sense of security through lying—the biblical security of a gentle and quiet spirit.

LET'S PRAY:

"Lord God, Thank You for being merciful to me when I fall short in my parenting and for loving me unconditionally! I want to honor You by treating my children the way You treat me. Lord, if I have embittered and frustrated my child, please forgive me and help me to change! Help us to begin afresh and to build trust with one another. Father, remove any falsehood from the lips of my son and convict him when he tells me a lie. Give me Your knowledge and wisdom to deal with this foothold in our home, and break every chain that would bind us and weaken our relationships. Thank You, God, that we can have victory through Christ! In Jesus' name, amen!"

Amber

CHAPTER 10: MANIPULATION

I looked ridiculous. There I was, trying to get my toddler to leave the park, and with every step closer to him, he ran in a zig-zag path away from me toward the swing set. I wanted one thing. He wanted another.

Earlier, I watched as a teenager sulked on a bench outside his school, arms crossed, hoodie pulled tightly to frame his sour-looking face. His mother wouldn't allow him to go with his friends to a baseball game until he mowed their lawn, and he was determined to make her miserable by his moody silent treatment.

And then there was the little girl who kept asking, "But, WHY?" every time her mother told her that she couldn't have something on the shelf at Target. Eventually, she dissolved into alligator tears and quivering lips as her mom wrenched the coveted doll from her grasp.

Manipulation can take the form of questioning our authority, whining, withholding affection, criticisms, crying, backtalk, procrastination, and false accusations. The goal of every manipulator is the same: to control. Its root? Selfishness. The issue for us as moms is that we must not have the same sinful root of selfishness for our own gain, therefore unwittingly modeling manipulation ourselves.

In His day, Jesus faced manipulators on many occasions recorded in Scripture, and we can learn from His divine responses. Consider Proverbs 26:4: "Do not answer a fool according to his folly, or you yourself will be just like him" (NIV). As moms, if we respond to our kids in the same way that they are trying to manipulate or control us, then we are sinning ourselves and even manipulating them to get our own way, instead of lovingly pointing them to Christ with godly responses.

Take a look at what Lou Priolo says about this in his book, *Heart of Anger*:

"Christ never answered a fool with a foolish response. He never fought folly with folly. In communicating with fools, He never employed communication forms that violated Scripture. Although He did respond to foolishness, He did not respond in kind. In other words, He did not allow the fool with whom He was talking to drag Him down to his level by playing the same sinful communication games as His opponent."[3]

If your child yells at you, do you resort to yelling back? Have you ever dissolved into a puddle of tears in the middle of an argument with your child? Are you tempted to walk away in exasperation and give your child the cold shoulder as an act of punishment for their behavior? Do you accuse your son or daughter of wrongdoing before you have really even listened to see what the bickering is all about? Have you ever become angry because they are embarrassing you, rather than grieving that they are sinning against God?

If we want God to bless us in our parenting, we need to be careful that we are not modeling manipulation for our own needs—kids who behave the way we want them to. Instead, we need to patiently reveal to them their responsibility, and point them towards Godly behavior. Jesus did this in Scripture on many occasions, often by doing two things:

1. He pointed out the manipulator's responsibility.

And,

2. He spoke truth from Scripture.

Instead of chasing my child around the park like a maniac, I can respond like Christ with dignity and composure. I can say to my child, "Son, you know that the right response is to say, 'Okay, Mommy' and to obey when I ask you to do something." I'm reminding him, lovingly and calmly, of what he already knows is my expectation, because I practiced this response with him in advance. And then, I speak the truth to him in love by saying, "Remember, Jesus promises that if you want to enjoy a long life, then you are to listen and obey your parents. I want things to go well for you, so come with me now." I then offer him a couple of acceptable choices

IN THE MIDDLE OF THE CONFLICT IS NOT ALWAYS THE BEST TIME TO SPEAK THE TRUTH IN LOVE.

so that he feels a sense of ownership and control instead of becoming embroiled in another round of battle, by saying, "You can either skip to the car, or I can race you there. Which would you like to do?"

We can sincerely empathize with our sulking teen by letting him know that we realize it's a disappointment that he can't go to the baseball game, but we appreciate that he honors his responsibility to us to mow the lawn. We leave the attitude choice up to him, and then follow up later with a kind and respectful conversation about heart attitudes.

When our kids are immature and they make a scene in the toy store, we don't have to get angry or embarrassed by their tears or give in and buy a new toy. We can give them a squeeze, and remind them that we will have fun at home with the dolls that we already own, opening up an opportunity to talk about contentment later in the day.

In the middle of the conflict is not always the best time to speak the truth in love. Sometimes, we need to have those conversations as a follow-up, when their hearts are more receptive; but the key is to be calm, consistent, and focused on the goal of pointing our kids to Christ, instead of letting loose an emotional response or engaging in our own adult brand of sinful manipulation.

If we resort to raising our voices, profanity, criticism, physical abuse, or sinful anger, then we need to take a step back and ask the Lord to forgive us for giving in to sinful responses. We may need to go back to the drawing board and coach our kids through our reasonable expectations, and then pray for self-control and wisdom when they fall short, so that we respond calmly and lovingly by pointing out their responsibility and then drawing their hearts to Christ. Otherwise, we alienate them by our unfair treatment and provoke them to anger.

Ultimately, we can't control the hearts of our children. The Holy Spirit must do the convicting, and therefore, we don't have to take their sinfulness personally. Nor do we need to respond as if we are being attacked. Rather, if we love them as Christ loves them, we can recognize that their misuse of control is a sin issue that we can help them navigate with consistency and truth.

Moms, we can remain steadfast in the face of manipulation as our hearts turn towards compassion for our children in their struggles to overcome self. Take joy today in knowing that these conflicts are not about you. They are an opportunity to champion the heart of your child towards righteousness; rejoice in the knowledge that God has equipped you for this awesome job. Overcome your child's corrupt motives by your biblical influence, and expect God's blessings to be a holy manipulation of your heart and theirs.

LET'S PRAY:

"Heavenly Father, when my child is being manipulative, I don't want to resort to my own foolish responses. God, I need You to help me remain calm and consistent. Lord, help me to approach my child's sinfulness with godly authority that is cloaked in grace. I feel my own emotions rise to dangerous levels when my child is trying to control me or a situation. I need Your peace to rule my heart in these heated moments! I don't want to act like a fool, nor do I want my children to be foolish. Help my kids to set aside foolish things as they mature, and help me to grow spiritually in these tense moments. Lord, You are powerful and able to meet me right where I am—thank You for being an ever-present help in time of need! In Jesus' name, amen!"

Amber

CHAPTER 11: ADHD, AUTISM, DYSLEXIA, OCD, APD, ODD

•••

Do you have a child with impulse control issues, ADHD, Oppositional Defiance Disorder, Aspergers, Autism, Dyslexia, APD, Depression, Anxiety, or a unique concoction of those listed above? And is it hard? I bet it is. I know it is. **Having a child with special needs, behavioral disorders, and learning difficulties can be one of the most difficult weights to bear. And under the pressure, moms can explode, marriages implode, and love erode.** It's all so very complicated.

One sweet mom recently asked for prayer concerning her anger, and was so insightful to recognize the connection between the constant energy her child with unique needs requires and her own twitchy trigger finger. She confessed the way she tends to explode at the rest of the family when she is simply worn out by her one special child.

Yes. I can relate. I remember going to the psychiatrist after my son was diagnosed with ADHD. After he was assessed, I immediately started talking about all the other issues in our family and the possible disorders my other kids might have. The doctor smiled, nodded, and said, "It's very possible nobody else has any diagnosable issues. They have issues, but the sort of issues that come from proximity. Don't worry. Let's see if we can help this one kid first. Usually what happens is that once we help one child with impulse control and oppositional tendencies, everyone else's behavior in the home begins to change."

Kids with behavioral, developmental, or learning issues often cause the whole family to have issues as well. For example, if one child is hyperactive, discontent, or argumentative, think of the way it affects siblings and Mom and Dad. That peaceful home you always imagined transforms into a stressful one with terse replies and a short-tempered marriage.

Unfortunately, it's not as easy as a little pill.

HAVING A CHILD WITH SPECIAL NEEDS, BEHAVIORAL DISORDERS, AND LEARNING DIFFICULTIES CAN BE ONE OF THE MOST DIFFICULT WEIGHTS TO BEAR. AND UNDER THE PRESSURE, MOMS CAN EXPLODE, MARRIAGES IMPLODE, AND LOVE ERODE.

Some challenges simply aren't so treatable, and the ramifications run deep and wide. Sure, we can learn behavior modification techniques and coping skills, seek the help of therapists, try changing their diet, and seek homeopathic remedies or more traditional medications, but for many families there remain...challenges. Challenges because of that one dear child who sits awkwardly somewhere on the spectrum, demanding much of our time, every waking moment. Or the kid with dyslexia that comes home with two hours of homework each school night, along with a backpack full of self-loathing. And by the time you get his needs taken care of, you are all poured out—stressed, sad, and short tempered too.

I'm sorry.

I'm sorry that you have such a challenging reality. But here's the deal, my friends: Your charge to love is the same as the woman next door with two compliant girls and bumper stickers boasting, "My child was on the honor roll...Again!" Every Christian has been given the same commission, regardless of circumstance: to love, because we have first been loved, and to forgive, because Christ first forgave us. We are exhorted to suffer beside our children as long as need be, because our God is long-suffering in His tender care toward us.

I was a child when I first saw the film, *"What's Eating Gilbert Grape."* I remember the scene when Gilbert (Johnny Depp) snaps under the pressure of caring for his brother Arnie (Leonardo DiCaprio), who has a developmental delay. He slams his little brother around and shoves him harshly into the bathtub. It's a painful and emotionally confusing scene to watch, because you don't just care for little Arnie, you care for his big brother too. He's abusing from a place of carrying too heavy a load.

Some of you are in that place. Hopefully you aren't physically harming your children, but it's possible to be verbally assaulting them and emotionally abusing them. If you are harming them in any way, I encourage you to seek help from someone who loves you and your family. Get counseling to deal with your anger and frustration, and learn new tools to care for your special kid.

Believe it or not—experience it or not—we have all received good and not evil from the Father's hand. But good doesn't always mean easy. I believe good means just the right circumstances to help us recognize our desperate need for Jesus each and every hard day! That child with Aspergers and the two with ADHD, the teenager who struggles with anxiety, the one with OCD and his brother with APD, the husband weighed down heavy with depression, and you with your own soul sadness: every human issue has the ability to point us towards our deepest soul need. We need God's power in our weakness, His saving in our failures, His hand to hold us up, His love when ours runs bone dry.

Ladies, there is no formula to persevere gracefully through these challenges, and every other, other than Christ in you, each and every day. As you abide in Him morning by morning, ask Him to give you very specific wisdom about how to raise the children He gave you. When I think of parenting difficult children, I think of Solomon, king over Israel. He knew that the holy job set before him was too much for him to do with his own understanding. And so, when God graciously offered to give him anything, King David's son asked for wisdom. Wisdom. He could have asked for peace, but he asked for wisdom. He could have asked for riches, but he asked for wisdom. He could have asked for ease and happiness, but he asked for wisdom.

God was so blessed by Solomon's answer, He vowed to give wisdom along with every other good thing Solomon did not ask for. It was, and remains today, God's very favorite prayer when we are leading others. And isn't that what parenting is —leading, governing God's people?

"Give me wisdom and knowledge, that I may lead this people, for who is able to govern this great people of yours?" (2 Chronicles 1:10, NIV)

We need wisdom as we lead these little ones, who belong to God. Wisdom about medicine and wisdom about diets, wisdom about what we are to say and how we are to say it, wisdom about education, and wisdom about how to discipline them that they might learn to be self-disciplined (though they battle impulse-control issues!). We need wisdom to understand what it means to let love cover a multitude of their challenging sins—so that we don't react with sins of own. We need wisdom. I need wisdom.

"The words of a man's mouth are deep waters; the fountain of wisdom is a bubbling brook." (Proverbs 18:4)

I sat with my child on the end of his bed one afternoon when math was swirling in his head and simply would not make sense. He asked me, "Why do I have this issue?" And I hung my head in surrender there beside him.

"Son," I simply said, "we all have issues. Every single person under heaven has challenges in their lives. And God has allowed them so that we can learn to turn to Him for His strength to get through each difficult day." And then I shared with him a few of my own challenges, because he needed flesh-and-blood proof that he wasn't alone. I told him all about how I rode the short bus to school early in the morning for my remedial reading classes; I told him about my trips to the school therapist because I thought I was dumb; and I told him that they considered holding me back in the fourth grade because multiplication and adjectives made no sense to me.

God gave me the wisdom I needed in that moment, as we sat at the foot of his bed. Then we talked about God's Word, His faithfulness and His love. How much better...how much better than if I had let his issues cause ugly, graceless issues of my own.

Do you have a child whose challenges challenge you? Do their issues create issues in your own heart? And is their developmental delay stunting your own spiritual development?

I have no doubt that you have read all the latest research and visited with every specialist you could find. Maybe what you need most is to simply ask the Lord for His wisdom in the midst of it all.

LET'S PRAY:

"Dear Lord, please give me the wisdom I need to lead this great people of Yours. Though their challenges challenge me, let Your grace drip from my lips, be the tenderness in my touch, and shine like kindness from my eyes. Supernaturally transform me, Lord, into a tangible reflection of Your gentleness in the face of every adversity. Yes, Lord, give me wisdom and give me grace—today, tomorrow, and the next day, and the next day, and the next... until Your wisdom and Your grace become my own. Amen"

Wendy

CHAPTER 12: VIDEO GAME ADDICTION

Along with my son's recent birthday came new video games for his XBOX 360.

The video game world is new to us—our oldest was nearly 8 before we allowed him any kind of gaming, and that was just this year. We often set time limits on their video games, and Sundays are our screen-free days.

Still, it didn't take long for us to experience first-hand the effects of gaming—changes in attitude (not the good kind!), begging and pleading when we have already set a limit to how long they could play, arguing over taking turns, and general fit throwing when it came time to put the controllers down.

Any of this sound familiar?

My kids' reactions stirred up frustration in my own heart. I saw that electronics could easily derail our goal for unity and peace in our home. What I quickly began to realize is that, in my sons' immaturity, gaming was becoming an idol. They cared more about video games than anything else. I was beginning to wonder where my sweet boys went! It seemed like gaming was winning out over our values as a family. I didn't like the fact that it could easily become a trigger towards anger and frustration for all of us.

As their mom, I knew that I needed to set some reasonable boundaries—not because I needed to control my kids with an iron fist, but because they simply were not capable of seeing the harm their behavior was causing in our family relationships between them as siblings, and towards Mom and Dad.

We have a little mantra at our house: Relationships first, stuff second. *In other words, no material thing is more important than preserving fellowship in our family.*

When we release parental control over the remote controller, we set ourselves up for conflict. If something we are involved in or obsessing over is harming a relationship, then we have to deal with it right away. We decided to hold a rare family meeting to lay out

RELATIONSHIPS FIRST, STUFF SECOND.

some new ground rules, and, more importantly, relate why we were doing so. I'm going to share with you what we decided to do in case you are feeling that you need to take a similar plunge.

Here's what we did when we needed to pull back on gaming devices:

Prepare Them

The night before, we let them know that we were going to have a family meeting the next day. We weren't doom and gloom about it; we just wanted them to know that it was going to be an important time for us to talk about some "family stuff." They nodded their heads—*fine by them.*

Lay a Foundation with a Positive Tone

First, we approached the conversation with an upbeat and positive attitude, not a serious, scolding tone, lest we lose and alienate our audience from the get-go. Then we reviewed Ephesians 6:1-3 to lovingly remind them that their role as kids is to obey Mom and Dad because God, in His love and wisdom, knows that obeying us will result in a long and enjoyable life. I had each boy take turns reading a verse or answering some simple questions to keep them engaged.

> *"Children, obey your parents in the Lord, for this is right.*
> *"Honor your father and mother" (this is the first*
> *commandment with a promise), "that it may go well with*
> *you and that you may live long in the land." (Ephesians*

6:1-3)

More head nodding. So far, so good.

Obey Mom and Dad because of our love for God? *Check.*

And because it will lead to an enjoyable life? *Check.*

New Guidelines

I then briefly explained that we were going to be doing something new for one month (mind you, it would stay in place in the future, but this month was our experimental time). We reminded ourselves that people are more important than things, and that playing outside, taking care of our bodies through exercise, and exploring the world around us was a way we could also honor God.

Then, we took the plunge.

Keeping my tone of voice upbeat, I explained that they would each earn 30 minutes after 3:00 PM every weekday to play an educational game or watch an educational YouTube video about a game. They could also play one of their favorite games, Just Dance, because it is physical and gets them exercising.

We explained that they could lose the privilege to play, but I would give them fair warning if that was about to happen. In general, I don't parent with a reward system because I don't want them to do the right thing to get something. **I want my children to do the right thing, because it's the right thing.** But I also don't want to remove games altogether at this point, and in this area, it seemed a reasonable approach.

I then explained that on Saturday morning, they could play entertaining games for an hour each. (It also meant that one of the gun-shooting games that I didn't think was appropriate for my son would be off limits for all of this month. I didn't share that in the family meeting because I knew it would be a big blow. I saved that conversation for a private talk with my oldest so that I could go into better detail and give him room to grieve over it while I focused on showing him empathy.)

Sundays would remain screen-free, as in the past.

The Reaction

There were a few brave tears as the impact of these new guidelines sank in, but they cheered up a bit when I explained that they we would be taking a special trip to a video game store to buy a used copy of a mom-approved game they had been wanting for some time. They would get to play the game that first Saturday! This helped ease the sting a bit— phew! Which leads to this important next step...

Set Them Up For Success

As the parent, you have to prepare yourself for a few days of complaining, kids being "bored," and general withdrawal-like symptoms. This part? Not fun, I won't lie. But, it's worth it—I promise! Don't take their frustrations personally or resort to your own irrational behavior. *Take it all in stride as you gently stick to your decision.* My kids and I both had to adjust, and it was important for me to set them up for success.

Here are a few things you can do to minimize whining:

- Swap out old toys from the garage and bring them inside or set up outdoor activities so they have some "new" things to play with.

- Plan a few play dates with friends, particularly outside at parks or at local pools, etc.

- Stop what you are doing more often to sit down with them to play board games, or do crafts and artwork.

- Implement a reading time where older kids read to younger ones.

- Offer constructive options to them before they begin to complain about being bored.

- Lovingly remind them when they are doing the right things that you are proud of them and excited that they are earning their time to play a game later that day.

Setbacks

One morning, my husband forgot about our new guidelines, and, sure enough, I came into the room to kids playing video games. We regrouped and got back on track. No harm, no foul! Don't let little hiccups or poor communication sabotage your new boundaries!

After only a week with our new guidelines, my boys began cooperating with one another again and a spirit of unity returned. Now, they play games with each other, use their imaginations, and go outside to play on the swing set! I call that success!

If you feel a sink in your gut when you think about your own family's gaming habits, or you find that this is a trigger for your own anger, why don't you join us in setting limits?

Don't let your fear of your kids' reactions keep you from parenting them well! Instead of reacting with irritation or becoming hopeless over gaming, we can simply set fair expectations and stick to them with consistency. Setting healthy boundaries for immature kids isn't always fun and games, but it creates room for healthy relationships, and that is a win-win for all.

LET'S PRAY:

"Dear Lord, I don't want anything to be a master over my children, except Your Holy Spirit. Setting boundaries for my kids can be hard. Lord, help me to be lovingly consistent as I seek to limit the impact of technology in my home. Work in the hearts of my children, that they may honor the parameters I have implemented for them. Help me to be compassionate towards them and help me to be wise when there are setbacks. Lord, rule over our home so that we become a family who is in tune with Your Holy Spirit's leading. Remove any idols from our lives so that we can give you the place in our hearts that You deserve! In Jesus' name, amen!"

Amber

CHAPTER 13: OVER-STIMULATION

....

I walked into the sterile room with florescent lights, and draped an extra blanket over the top of my sleeping baby's stroller. Only four weeks old, he slept most of every day (thoughtfully preserving his strength for our midnight bonding sessions). We waited so long for the pediatrician I eventually fell asleep in the exam room's plastic blue chair, slumped over like a worn rag doll. When the doctor walked in, I startled awake and smiled awkwardly. He nodded like I wasn't the first new mom to doze off waiting on him.

Over the next ten minutes, he asked me a litany of questions about how the baby was sleeping and feeding and pooping. He worked his way through a clipboard list of details as he roused my baby to count his fingers and toes. One particular question surprised me.

"Did you hang a mobile over your baby's crib?"

"Of course."

"Does it have bright colors, flashing lights, and a happy melody?" He prodded deeper.

"Yes," I proudly nodded.

He then jotted down a note on his prescription pad and handed it to me. It read: "Take down the mobile until your child is 9 months old."

I read it then laughed aloud, surprised.

My baby's doctor laughed with me because he was a jovial man with a loud tie, and crumbs on his mustache. But then he said, "Your child has had nothing exciting him for nine long months. Nothing but warm, quiet, rest. Just the right environment for a baby to grow in, don't you agree? Then suddenly, he was born into the bright lights of this big world and we immediately want to stimulate and entertain him constantly. But he has his whole life ahead of him for that. How about, instead, you just give this little fella nine more peaceful months? Just nine more months of dim lights without all the bells and whistles? Doesn't that sound relaxing?"

Exhausted, I couldn't help but agree.

A year or two later, when my first-born was still very young and his little brother was the newborn, I read an article about the benefits and dangers of TV watching for young children. The one point that stuck with me most built upon the advice of my children's pediatrician. It spoke of over-stimulating our children's minds. Most television shows (and gaming devices too) can over-stimulate a child because of how quickly and constantly the images change. Quick edits back and forth between scenes, color and sound flashing and popping, zooming in and zooming out, then cutting over to another exciting close-up followed by a whole new song and dance... a toddler's eyes and brain bounce around so fast their little beings get all shaken up!

And then we ask them to stay still in our laps as we read them a quiet

A MOM MUST GUARD HER OWN QUIET HEART BEFORE SHE CAN TEND TO THE OVER-STIMULATED HEARTS OF HER CHILDREN.

story, sit still at the dinner table for a calm meal, remain by our side as we walk to the park, and look us in the eye when they answer our questions...but they're still bouncing! Not listening; ignoring, disrespecting, disobeying. Or maybe, they're just over-stimulated.

And maybe we are too.

Just the way that funny old pediatrician gave me a prescription for my child's emotional and neurological health, I want to encourage you to protect your own body and mind from over-stimulation during this exhausting season.

A mom must guard her own quiet heart before she can tend to the over-stimulated hearts of her children.

Do you ever feel like your children are constantly pushing your buttons until the sirens go off and you start hollering? Their wrong behavior, constant crying, hitting, complaining, needing snacks, mess making, nap fighting... it's your undoing. However, what if they're not really trying to push your buttons at all? What if your buttons are just all stressed out because you're over-stimulated and over-tired? Maybe your buttons are super sensitive because they need more dark hours every day. Maybe you need some more time in a less stimulating environment so that you can stay calm and kind and respond the right way. Maybe you're just over-stimulated.

Some days I bounce between my never-ending to-do list— dropping older children off at school; running to the library with the littles for story-hour; then to the grocery store before naps, checking my cell phone umpteen times at red lights. Then, we head home to change out another load of laundry before getting lunch and tucking the baby into bed. Coming downstairs, tripping over Legos, the preschoolers and I dive into making homemade bubbles, then we trace letters together, followed by a show so I can prep dinner, fold some clothes, make a call, and wake the baby to go get the big kids from school. Then off to soccer practice, and doling out snacks for the little ones while the big ones play. Plugging in ear buds, I listen to a podcast as I push the youngest on a swing. Then we hurry home for dinner making, with the sound of the television in the background. We have dinner and devotionals at the table, but everyone's bouncing and talking and complaining...so I get angry! Exhausted physically and emotionally, but more than anything else...I'm simply over-stimulated.

So what can we do when children need to get to school and soccer practice and you have preschoolers wanting to play and a baby needing a nap and another trip to the grocery store to make? How do we keep ourselves resting in quiet spaces, when there aren't any? We must make some: carve them out and protect them.

Three ways to cultivate quiet hearts in the over-stimulating season of motherhood

Sound

Keep the music and the TVs turned off for most of the day. That constant background hum isn't white noise, lulling us to sleep, but a static buzz crossing our signals and keeping us agitated. Want to listen to music in the car? Go for it! Want a movie with your husband after the kids go down? Enjoy it! But don't let the noise fill every crevice all day long. I'm exhausted just thinking of it.

Devices

We are better at setting boundaries for our children on their devices than we are for ourselves. But our eyes and minds can bounce and grow weary just like theirs. So close your laptop and set down your phone. Try not to look at a screen for at least 30 minutes before you close your eyes at night. Flashing images stimulate your brain, but you need deep sleep so that you can be ready to love your people again fresh tomorrow. So power off and sleep well.

Quiet Time with the Lord

Just as our children need a break from the constant stimuli so they can learn to simply rest in the quiet of their rooms for a little while each day...so we need that quiet space. The opposite of over-stimulation is rest. Rest. Slowing down, being still, and knowing the Prince of Peace. Find time and space to rest each day. Meet with Him, talk with Him, and hear from Him. Let Him calm you down, swaddle you up tight, and remove some of the mobiles dangling over our ever-moving life.

When our children get over-stimulated, they can be little terrors, no doubt. But when we are over-stimulated, agitated on the inside, we can be the most terrible of all, because we can't cope with them in loving ways. Don't you see? Our over-stimulation is more our trigger here than theirs!

Therefore, we must learn to find balance in the quiet places of our faith lives, though our family lives are busy. We must learn to cultivate quiet spaces in our daily routines without the constant buzz of podcasts and Pandora. We must turn off the stimulating mobiles, spinning over our heads and hyping us up. We're the adults, and our toddlers need us calm.

Let us learn with our children to turn off the background music, the devices, and the car... and be home... and be still... and be calm.

LET'S PRAY:

"Dear Lord, I do get overwhelmed by the constant noise and all the going. And just like my children, I can get over-stimulated by too much screen-time as well. Would you help me, Lord, to set boundaries around and within my days so that I am not jittery and easily triggered? You are both the Fortress that I run into for my peace, and the Peace which fills me from within. Too marvelous! Help me to remember that when I feel short-tempered and shaken. I ask this in the powerful, storm-quieting name of Jesus. Amen."

Wendy

CHAPTER 14: IRRESPONSIBLE BEHAVIOR

....

I have a confession to make. I didn't do my first load of laundry until I was well into college. I never had required chores growing up. And yet, I am a driven adult with a strong work ethic. In the absence of chore charts with animal stickers or requiring summer jobs for us as teenagers to earn money, the one thing my parents did extremely well was model hard work.

I was expected to lend a hand at whatever task was before me, and there was a pervasive attitude that you did things right the first time or kept trying until it was as good as you could get it.

Now that I have my own family, we use a similar approach. My boys know that the general expectation in our home is, **"See a need, fill a need."** I expect my boys to follow through on tasks on their own once they have been taught: things like putting their dishes in the sink, filling the dog's water bowl when it gets empty, and putting their shoes in the basket by our front door. They all know that when we leave a room, we turn the lights out, and that either brother can help buckle the baby of the family into his car seat.

We don't partition off zones for each kid to be in charge of, nor do we have an overarching system in place to reward or discipline our kids based on their performance. I think methods like these can be helpful, and there are many possibilities and arrangements that may fit your family dynamics. We will talk about some of those in a moment. **But one thing that should be true for all of us is our biblical approach to teaching our kids responsibility and our godly response when they fall short.**

Some of us believe that our kids will only obey us if we YELL AT THEM. But that's simply what we have trained them to do. Of course, I'm not talking simply about volume here—we would need to raise our voices if a child was heading into danger, like running into the street. But yelling at our kids as a way of getting them to do the things we want them to do is simply not a biblical response to our triggers.

Proverbs 29:11 says, "A fool gives full vent to his spirit, but a wise man quietly holds it back." Moms who scream and let their words tumble out unchecked are considered foolish. We can feel the tension mounting, yet still be like the wise man who "quietly holds it back" and finds a gracious way to communicate. It will take time and patience to turn this around, but it's absolutely possible!

Foundationally, it's up to us as the parents to teach and train outside of times of chaos or in the aftermath of conflict. This is especially true when it comes to messes our kids have made or when they don't do their designated chores. We don't need to get embroiled in an argument or lose our tempers over laziness. Nor do we need to scream at them as if they can't hear us. When our kids are not fulfilling their responsibility, we simply need to keep doing the good parenting—going back to the idea that we are coaching our kids towards success!

> ANGRY PUNISHMENTS CRUSH OUR CHILDREN'S SPIRITS, BUT LOVING CONSEQUENCES CORRECT THEIR HEARTS.

Here are a few tips and reminders that will help you remain in a position of loving authority while training your kids to do the things you ask of them:

1.**Keep in mind that the goal is to let the kids feel the weight of the natural consequences that come with irresponsibility.** Loving consequences look very different from mean-spirited or angry punishments. **Angry punishments crush our children's spirits, but loving consequences correct their hearts.**

2. **Give them choices.** "Ron, your sports gear is washed and ready in the laundry room. Please put it in your gym bag and

load it into the car sometime before you go to bed tonight so it's ready to go to football practice with you in the morning. If you don't do so, I'll do it for you, but you will have to pay me to do it. I'll take that money out of your allowance for next week if you don't have the money to pay me tomorrow, but I'm sure you'll do it yourself before bedtime anyway. Thanks, Buddy!" Then, walk away and let Ron be responsible. If he is irresponsible, then the natural consequence of paying Mom to do the job will come into play without the arguing or angry flare ups.

3. Make the most of your kids' eagerness to be helpers. When they are younger, you can spur them to action by saying things like, "Hmmm, I know I have 3 awesome helpers here today and there are windows that need washing. I wonder who is going to volunteer to do an amazing job cleaning with me. We might have to cool off afterwards with a popsicle!"

4. Make it into a game. I often time my kids with a stopwatch to see who can pick up at least 10 toys and put them in their proper places in 30 seconds or less. Don't forget to blast upbeat music while you are at it—when the music ends, time is up!

5. Use calm and sincere consistency in place of arguing. When my kids begin to protest, I simply say, "I know. It's not always easy to do the right thing. I'm sorry you are feeling so crummy about it. Now go ahead and clean your room. You can do it now, or in 20 minutes." Repeat this dialogue again and again, if necessary.

Eventually, if the arguing and resisting continues, you can say something like, "It sounds like you aren't able to really hear what I am saying. Why don't you go ahead and have some time in your room to think about a way I can help you understand the importance of obeying and cleaning your room? I have some ideas, but I'd like to hear yours first. I'll come talk with you in about 30 minutes when I'm done ironing. If you don't have any appropriate ideas about how we can fix this situation, we will use my ideas—but they may be less appealing to you."

6. Study your child as an individual and see what motivates them. For some, it will be words of affirmation, so praise them as a starting point to lead into chores. For others, it will be quality time—they like to do things with others, so offer them chores that they can do with a partner or with you. Notice what makes them tick and then play off of their unique strengths!

7. Choose realistic jobs. Some larger families with older kids have zones that they manage and then rotate. That way, each child gets experience in all aspects of maintaining a home: cleaning bathrooms, helping prep for dinner, or taking care of pets. Emphasize a team spirit and foster a sense of togetherness as you all chip in to help one another.

8. Remind your kids the reasoning behind working hard and being responsible: "Whatever you do, work at it with all your heart, as working for the Lord, not for human masters, since you know that you will receive an inheritance from the Lord as a reward. It is the Lord Christ you are serving." (Colossians 3:23-24) Let's model this work ethic in our own lives, too. Even the patient process of training our kids in responsibility should be an act of worship!

9. Don't take away past rewards. In general, I don't think it's a good practice to remove rewards already earned or to renege on promises. This discourages a kid who worked hard for that incentive in the first place. If they earned something, keep it in place and use other methods to reach their hearts, instead of demerits that will simply make them angry with you and motivate them to give up trying. The Bible reminds us in Ephesians 6:4, "Fathers, do not exasperate your children; instead, bring them up in the training and instruction of the Lord," (NIV). We don't want to provoke our kids to anger and this is a surefire way to do just that.

10. Let them do it their way. It's tempting for a mom to hover and correct, but there is a difference between loving and helpful input and micro-managing. If this is an issue for you, learn to let it go. Give your kids space to mature and become proficient in their chores. Affirm the parts they do well.

Responsible kids don't just happen. It's up to us to train our kids and to lay a foundation of truth that serving the Lord often looks like mopping the floors or feeding the cat. At the end of the day, our kids will answer to the Lord for their part, but for the angry mom, the only thing better than a child's clean room is her own clean conscience.

LET'S PRAY:

"Dear Jesus, I want everything I do to be an act of worship. Give my children hearts that desire to serve joyfully, too! I know that chores can be a struggle and that responsible kids don't happen overnight, but Lord, help me to be patient with them while I train them. You are creative, so allow me to be creative in the ways I teach responsibility. May my own willingness to do everything with joy influence my kids. When I'm weary, Lord, strengthen me. Make our family a team who pitches in to help one another out of loving-kindness. Thank You for being our strength when we are weak and for giving us purpose, even in simple things like chores. In Your Name I pray, amen!"

Amber

CHAPTER 15: WHEN WILL THEY EVER CHANGE?

Why do marriage and motherhood have to be so hard? When we got engaged, our eyes were fixed on happily ever after. Even though we vowed "in sickness and health," the dream was health and happiness. Though we swore to love one another "for better or for worse," we naively expected a whole lot more "better" than "worse." The same is true when we wanted babies. Whether conceiving was as easy as your wedding night, or as difficult as a long barren season followed by a trip across the ocean to an orphanage, the idea was happiness and the completion of a dream. And the dream was good. But many women I know would describe their reality today more like a nightmare with unruly kids who simply won't change.

Long days with three children under the age of five, with nobody taking naps; complaining about what's been served for dinner; throwing fits at home and having meltdowns in public; and their daddy works long hours and comes home late and tired, with very little left over to contribute emotionally. You do your best to be consistent when it comes to love and discipline, believing whole-heartedly that in due season, you will reap if you do not grow weary and lose heart. And yet your heart is quivering right along with your bottom lip, because there's still no fruit. *When will they ever change?*

You see other children who walk with their mother through the grocery store without begging and crying, hitting a sibling, or begging for a phone. You have friends whose children are actually pleasant to be around and can carry on a mature conversation, while yours are interrupting and whining to go home. Why were you given a loud and impulsive son, an argumentative teenager who acts like a victim, multiple children with special needs, a daughter whose fits absolutely wear you out? "Is it ever going to change? Are *they* ever going to change?"

> WHILE WE FOCUS ON OUR CHILDREN'S LACK OF MATURITY, GOD IS EVER FOCUSED ON MATURING US!

Here at the end of this first section, focusing on the things our children do that trigger our anger, I want to ask the Lord what He might have purposed and planned for our maturity in light of their childish behavior. **While we focus on our children's lack of maturity, God is ever focused on maturing us!**

After a long day with two toddlers and a newborn babe, I drifted between waking and sleeping. The infant child at my breast was pulling slowly and I knew his swallows couldn't be rushed. In the quiet of the midnight hours I wondered when it would get easier. These words flooded my mind: "Consider it all joy, my brethren, when you encounter various trials, knowing that the testing of your faith produces endurance. And let endurance have its perfect result, so that you may be perfect and complete, lacking in nothing." (James 1:2-4)

This was the Bible verse I had memorized as a child—the one I never truly understood until my own personal trials hit me hard. When I was young and spiritually immature, I knew these verses had something to do with the Refiner's fire, perfecting us in the hot places of perseverance, but I didn't understand why God would choose such a painful method when He could simply make it all better: fix what's broken, heal what's sick, cure our disease, and eradicate our problems.

In my naiveté, I wanted God to grow me up in my comfortable life, through happy little Bible studies, and in my familiar pew at church on Sunday mornings. But as I rocked and nursed, it occurred to me that God uses rough sandpaper to make His creations lovely and smooth. And I knew, after a day where I had exploded over my little one's immaturity, that God was using their rough edges to smooth me out and soften my heart. **God planned the lion's share of my spiritual growth to be done in the fiery furnace of family life.**

When I was just a newly-wed, I read the book *Sacred Marriage* by Gary Thomas. The question he posed from the tagline on the cover was, "What if God designed marriage to make us holy more than to make us happy?"[4] It was a clever question, but didn't resonate with me at the time, as I was still euphoric in the honeymoon phase of our love affair. However, within a few short years, we had moved across the country, had three strong-willed little boys, and were both overwhelmed by the challenges of our blessed life together. There, a variation of the words from the cover of that book came back to me: What if God designed *motherhood* to make me holy rather than to make me happy? What a thought!

Gary Thomas went on in his book to suggest that family life was designed by God to be the *laboratory* where our holiness is cultivated.

Back at the beginning of my marriage, when all the young couples around us started having their first children, I would write James 1:17 on the inside of each baby shower card. "Every good and perfect gift is from above, coming down from the Father of lights." (James 1:17, NASB) It was a lovely sentiment, though I didn't know a thing about the Lord's precious little gifts at the time.

I do now.

Twelve years into this parenting marathon, I understand this Scripture a little better than I did back then. I have come to read the word "perfect" as an active verb, not a decorative adjective describing a noun. When we are pregnant, we imagine that the gift God is giving us is the child within our womb. But it turns out that that precious soul, and your marriage too, is simply a tool by which our perfecting happens. And that is the gift that The Father of lights intended from the beginning: To make us holy. That perfect gift, swaddled, is the perfecting tool that will bring us to maturity.

Our little gifts are darling little babes, complete with a sin nature and personality that tend to rub us wrong at times. God uses them like sandpaper in His tender hands. Back and forth against our spiritual lives, He rubs them purposefully, to smooth out our own sin tangles, to even out the selfish bumps, to smooth away our anger as we lean into God's rhythmic, loving refining.

Our children are not perfect, but they are perfectly designed to perfect us into the image of Christ. Isn't that amazing, and doesn't it shift our single-minded focus off of their foolishness and onto our own? We need to let go of this idea of 'perfect.' We don't have perfect children, perfect marriages, or perfect homes. But we do have a good and loving God who is passionate about the process of His perfecting plan in our homes. Doesn't that give you courage to press on and endure? Knowing that He is not a hands-off God? These painful trials have not slipped through His fingers and into our lives by accident—they've been purposefully placed there by the King over heaven and earth. Your trials and your children were not just allowed—they were anointed. Therefore, we are blessed.

"Blessed is the man who remains steadfast under trial, for when he has stood the test he will receive the crown of life, which God has promised to those who love him." James 1:12

Moms and dads, husbands and wives, persevere under your present trials. Surrender this maddening pursuit of perfect children, and seek how the Lord wants to perfect you in the midst of the challenges today. When will they ever change?

They will change, as will you, one perfecting day at a time.

LET'S PRAY:

"Dear Lord, I often forget that You are sovereign and kind when life feels abrasive, even painful. However, when I get really quiet, I remember that You have good and not evil planned for Your people. I'm one of Your people. My kids are Your people too. And You are our God. You have promised a

future of hope and not harm, even when our circumstances are uncomfortable. You have promised to bring us to completion—all of us. I don't think, Lord, that You are a hands-off God; I believe, instead, that You are very near and not surprised by our slow-going transformation. Every breath, every day, is an anointed part of Your plan to make us holy. To make us more like Your Son. So help me, help us, Lord. Amen."

Wendy

SECTION TWO: INTERNAL TRIGGERS

WHEN IT HAS EVERYTHING TO DO WITH US...

We have already focused on the obvious things our children do that trigger our inappropriate reactions. Learning to respond biblically, rather than in our own flesh anger, is our main focus here. We have come to the conclusion that God is more concerned with maturing us, in the fiery furnace of family life, than making sure our children are compliant and calm. While we stress out over our children's lack of maturity, God is focused on maturing us! He uses their rough edges to rub us smooth, like sandpaper in the hand of the master builder, that we might look more like Him.

As we begin section two of this collection of triggers, we're shifting gears a bit: Taking our eyes off of the things they do to set us off, and focusing instead on our own shortcomings, sin tendencies, hard-wiring, and personal trials that cause us to explode all over our little people.

Because, while some of our triggers have to do with them...most of our triggers have everything to do with us!

CHAPTER 16: LACK OF FAITH

....

In the hardest seasons of mothering, on my most difficult days, I have felt like a little boat tossed about on the waves. The storm was too big and I was too small. Having been raised in the church, I knew the story of Jesus and his disciples on the Sea of Galilee in the midst of a midnight storm: how the Messiah had been sleeping through it all, while his followers feared for their lives. Eventually, they shook Him awake, desperate for saving. And Jesus, peaceful and sure, "got up, rebuked the wind and said to the waves, 'Quiet! Be still!' Then the wind died down and it was completely calm. He said to his disciples, 'Why are you so afraid? Do you still have *no faith*?'" (Mark 4:39-40, NIV)

When I had my first child, I thought myself a woman of deep faith. And then the storm clouds gathered and the babies kept coming, and my hormones got all out of sorts. I felt shaky and unsure, and my marriage struggled as I cried. Overwhelmed by the powerful winds blowing in the wake of my three strong-willed toddlers, I didn't have a sense of the Lord's nearness—He seemed instead to be sleeping in the middle of my private squall! I had no sense of His presence or His peace.

On the days I feared the most, I questioned His love the most. As I questioned His love, my own love faltered. On the days my little vessel came closest to capsizing, my faith did, too. And as I cried salty tears, I watched the sea level rise. And the storm raged on; the storm about me and the storm within. Where was the Lord I was so sure that I believed in? And why wasn't He saving me from my inner turmoil and the tempest that threatened to be my undoing in these mothering years?

I knew that my lack of faith in the whirlwind was my biggest trigger. It had very little to do with my children and their childlike ways, and everything to do with my lack of faith. And again, another lesson from my childhood Bible flooded my heart. Jesus was surrounded by His followers and those curious to see Him perform another miracle, when a man pushed his way through the crowd and asked:

> *"Teacher, I brought you my son, who is possessed by a spirit that has robbed him of speech. Whenever it seizes him, it throws him to the ground. He foams at the mouth, gnashes his teeth and becomes rigid. I asked your disciples to drive out the spirit, but they could not."*

> *"You unbelieving generation," Jesus replied, "how long shall I stay with you? How long shall I put up with you? Bring the boy to me.' So they brought him. When the spirit saw Jesus, it immediately threw the boy into a*

convulsion. He fell to the ground and rolled around, foaming at the mouth.

Jesus asked the boy's father, "How long has he been like this?"

"From childhood," he answered. "It has often thrown him into fire or water to kill him. But if you can do anything, take pity on us and help us."

"'If you can'?" said Jesus. "Everything is possible for one who believes."

Immediately the boy's father exclaimed, "I do believe; help me overcome my unbelief!" (Mark 9:17-24, NIV)

In the middle of the storms, as the battles rage and illnesses threaten and childish behaviors blow at us with gale wind force, God is calling us to deeper faith! "Lord I believe, help my unbelief!"

"Then we will no longer be infants, tossed back and forth by the waves, and blown here and there by every wind of teaching and by the cunning and craftiness of people in their deceitful scheming." (Ephesians 4:14, NIV)

God made us for a very intimate relationship with Himself. He gave us the nearness of His Holy Spirit, that we might never walk through the storms alone. He is always in our boat. His Spirit indwells every person who has confessed their faith in Jesus Christ as their personal savior from sin. And once believed in, even with the smallest (mustard-seed size) measure of faith, God in all of His power rushes in, and takes up residency in the heart of the believer. But it doesn't stop there.

Daily, from trial to trial, from windstorm to windstorm, with whitecaps building beneath our little boats, He is there in the midst of those who believe.

God is our refuge and strength,
an ever-present help in trouble.
Therefore we will not fear, though the earth give way
and the mountains fall into the heart of the sea,
though its waters roar and foam
and the mountains quake with their surging.
There is a river whose streams make glad the city of God,
the holy place where the Most High dwells.
God is within her, she will not fall;
God will help her at break of day.
(Psalm 46:1-5, NIV)

Today's short chapter is chock-full of Scripture truth, to encourage your faith in the midst of your present storms. God's Word clearly promises in the story above that "anything is possible for those who believe." But conversely, "you must believe and not doubt, because the one who doubts is like a wave of the sea, blown and tossed by the wind." (James 1:6, NIV)

Does the imagery of being tossed about resonate with you during these parenting years? And may I ask, tenderly, if you have put your faith fully in Christ? Have you believed in your heart that Jesus is the Lord of your Life? Do you believe that He was sent by God to die for your sins, that you might be forever free and forgiven? And do you believe that God then raised His son from the dead, so that you might also be raised up into a new and eternal life? If you believe that this is true, and confess it with your lips, then you will be saved —both now and forevermore.

That does not, however, mean that life is suddenly without storms; but it is a promise that He will be with you, overcoming each one.

> *"I have told you these things, so that in me you may have peace. In this world you will have trouble. But take heart! I have overcome the world." (John 16:33, NIV)*

We will have storms. Maybe your anger is the biggest storm you are facing. That's a dangerous storm. Storms may threaten our peace, but we must hold tight to the Prince over our Peace, there in our small vessel. Hold tight to your faith, going deeper, holding stronger, confessing louder over the whirling of the winds as the storm rolls on.

Are you tossing about on the waves today? And is it possible your lack of peace has anything to do with your lack of faith? I wish that I could bow my head with you in this moment and cry out with you a prayer of belief. Of course, I can't do that on your behalf. Only you can surrender your fears and take hold of faith. If you have never done that, I invite you to put your faith in the only Savior, the One who has the power to stretch out His hand and calm the storms.

DAILY, FROM TRIAL TO TRIAL, FROM WINDSTORM TO WINDSTORM, WITH WHITECAPS BUILDING BENEATH OUR LITTLE BOATS, HE IS THERE IN THE MIDST OF THOSE WHO BELIEVE.

LET'S PRAY:

"Dear God, I am choosing in this moment to believe that You are the God who created the heavens and the earth, and You created me, too. I have done this life on my own long enough. I need You to save me from the storms that are raging around me and within me. I believe, Jesus, that You are the Son of God. I believe that You came to live a perfect, sinless life—a

life that I could never live—and then died for all the sin You never committed. I believe You died for my sin, too. And then, You rose from the dead; I believe that as well. And one day, when my life is over, I will be raised with You too. Not because of anything I did, but because I believed in what You did for me. I believe. I believe... please help my unbelief. Amen."

Wendy

CHAPTER 17: GENERATIONAL HABITS AND PATTERNS OF SIN

•••

I don't often talk about my own childhood, but I will say that I had to deal with the potential for the generational pattern of anger and yelling in my life as a new mom. My mom and dad grew up in a strict religious cult, and I was born about a year after they had been excommunicated from their church and shunned from their families and friends. So, I grew up under the umbrella of lives upended and with parents who had a long-entrenched pattern of unhealthy relationships and conflict. My parents are some of the most generous and thoughtful people I know, and they blessed my life by raising me in a solid Bible-teaching church that breathed life into my heart. But if ever there was a legacy of generational sin and a pattern of dysfunction, this was it. My family didn't even comprehend what a healthy environment looked like, having never experienced that for themselves.

So, how do I know that we don't have to repeat the patterns of our fathers and mothers? How do I know that God really does break the chains that bind? How do I know that we can be radically different parents than what was modeled for us? And how do I know that, even if we feel like we have "ruined" our kids, they can grow up to live out the best of what we were able to give them?

Because I'm living proof.

I didn't start losing my temper with my kids until my second son was born. I began reaching a breaking point over little things, started raising my voice, and often felt a deep sense of dread that I was becoming the mom I swore I would never be. I was carrying on the legacy of anger that had preceded me.

The Holy Spirit began to convict me. It took longer than I wanted it to, but I committed to repenting from my sin of pride, being quick to anger, and speaking harshly to my boys. I renewed my commitment to reading my Bible every day and spending time in prayer. Often, my only prayer was, *"Lord, I need you to stop my tongue from saying any word that does not build up those who listen. I don't want to hurt my kids or be an angry mom. Change my heart and make me a gentle mother! Father, forgive me, and give me the wisdom I need to glorify You. Break the generational chains!"*

More and more, I felt the Holy Spirit compelling me to take a deep breath, speak slowly and carefully to my children, and seek out ways to bless them with my words throughout the day. When my sons napped, I settled into my comfy chair and prioritized my spiritual growth as I read my Bible and Christian parenting books to help me deal with my sin issues.

I started apologizing to my boys and studying what it meant to be humble. Instead of focusing on the challenges in my life, I kept a gratitude journal, writing down all the big and small ways that I was blessed, and choosing to have a joyful heart. I asked the Lord to transform me by praying Psalm 51:10-12: "Create in me a clean heart, O God, and renew a right spirit within me. Cast me not away from Your presence, and take not Your Holy Spirit from me. Restore to me the joy of Your salvation, and uphold me with a willing spirit."

And God showed up, so I shaped up.

There was no magical overnight change. It was the slow realization that I was a new creation in Christ and that I didn't need to work hard to be different. I simply needed to own who I already was:

"Therefore, if anyone is in Christ, he is a new creation. The old has passed away; behold, the new has come." (2 Corinthians 5:17)

"I have been crucified with Christ. It is no longer I who live, but Christ who lives in me. And the life I now live in the flesh I live by faith in the Son of God, who loved me and gave himself for me." (Galatians 2:20)

Recognizing that Christ lives in us and will help us break every chain or pattern of sin is a blessing I took for granted.

The Holy Spirit transformation is the grace of God. It is the life-changing power of the Gospel that Wendy shared in the previous chapter. The legacy of new life in Christ is the one we get to pass on to our kids.

No generational sin is a match for the God of all generations.

Many moms have expressed to me their great sorrow and fear that their children will only remember them as angry, yelling moms. I want us to feel conviction for our sinful anger, but I also want those of us who have confessed our sin to stop looking over our shoulders into yesterday. Don't allow the Devil to convince you that your legacy is fixed.

Instead, dwell on how enriched your children's lives will be to see you model overcoming sin in your own life. Dwell on how they will be blessed

NO GENERATIONAL SIN IS A MATCH FOR THE GOD OF ALL GENERATIONS.

by witnessing what God can do in a heart that is His and with a life that is committed to doing what is right.

THAT is the real legacy you will leave, and it is beautiful!

Today is a day full of new mercies and opportunities to do the right thing, to respond with a gentle word, to cover sin with love, and to be a grace-filled mom and wife.

We all want to be moms who embody a gentle and quiet spirit, but it doesn't happen in one fell swoop. It happens minute-by-minute and moment-by-moment. The change in our hearts becomes more real and more secure each time we shimmy out of the old cloak of irritability and frustration and clothe ourselves with patience, kindness, and gentleness.

Today, look forward to your transformation. Refuse to gaze at your old self; as you develop patience towards your kids, offer it to yourself, too. Trust God to transform you, as He transformed me. Be filled with hope that the new memories you are impressing on the hearts of your children are the ones that will last.

Now, go into today and change your legacy!

LET'S PRAY:

"Father God, when You entered my heart, I became a new creation! No matter how much my past has affected me, I know that I do not have to repeat sinful patterns. Father, You are mighty and victorious in my life! Put to death any offensive way in me and revive me! Heal my heart, Lord! God, I do not want to carry into my future any behavior,

anger, bitterness, or strife from my past. Renew my heart and mind, that I may create a different kind of home-life for my child. Help me to leave a legacy of love and safety in my mothering that will carry on for many generations. Thank You for being a God of redemption and beauty! In Jesus' name, amen!"

Amber

CHAPTER 18: DEPRESSION, POST-PARTUM, HORMONAL IMBALANCE

••

There have been recent days when I just start shaking from joy on the inside and can't stop smiling. I mean, I make a bonafide fool of myself, talking to every lady picking over mangos and shallots at the grocery store, and the boy bagging my groceries looks at me sideways when I go on and on about those hazel eyes. I ask the older man in the electric shopping chair, who can't quite stand up tall enough to reach the bag of salted movie popcorn, if I can help. He says yes, so we continue together up and down the aisles, both of us smiling. And it feels good, for the man who is shorter than he once was, and for this woman who is taller than she was a year ago.

Not long ago, the Lord brought me out of depression's grip. The hold had been firm because her fingers were many— imbalanced hormones, adrenal fatigue, prolonged postpartum —all of them wrapped around my weary wrists like a vine with too many tendrils. I'd rip at one, but another was always growing up to take its place.

Today, however, there are smiles. Smiles spilling out and collecting like puddles at my feet, where tears used to pool.

I don't believe in formulas or cure-alls, but I do believe in the power of healthy conversation, in testimonies, and in a kind, redeeming God who reaches down into the muddiest, muckiest messes, smack-dab in our soul sadness, and pulls us up and out. Yeah, I believe in that stuff. And Kleenex, plenty of Kleenex. And gooey brownies, too.

How nice it would be to sit crisscross applesauce with you, pillows all around, a box of Kleenex to wipe away the tears when ugly-cries shake us something fierce, and brownies. Always brownies. But we can't do that, can we? Not really. So we gather here together, over printed words.

For Crying Out Loud!

If I were into formulas, equations that stated methodically that a + b = c, always, every time, then I'd start here. But depression is confusing. It's so stinkin' confusing that we whimper soft and alone, rather than CRYING OUT LOUD together. But, For Crying Out Loud, crying out is just what He wants to hear from us when we're hurting. Loud and bold and believing, "God, save me from this mess; I'm drowning in these tears."

> *"I waited patiently for the Lord; And He inclined to me and heard my cry. He brought me up out of the pit of destruction, out of the miry clay, And He set my feet upon*

a rock making my footsteps firm. He put a new song in my mouth, a song of praise to our God; Many will see and fear And will trust in the Lord." (Psalm 40:1-3, NIV)

This is the story of our Salvation. We were separated and desperate for saving, then in a moment we cried out, "God, I cannot do this alone." And that confession of faith in God's power was the key to unleashing His rescue plan for our lives. But here's the glorious truth we need in the darkest days this side of Heaven's hold: We still need saving. Here in this sin-drenched world, we remain actively in need of His powerful, rescuing arm.

••

GOD'S LIFTING HAND OFTEN LOOKS LIKE THE HANDS OF REAL PEOPLE ALL AROUND US.

••

Jesus said, "I have come that they might have life, and have it abundantly!" Those are two lives He came for: the life eternal and the life we're living now, full of abundant potential. So here's the confession: God, if You were strong enough to save me from sin and give me eternal life, You are most definitely able to save me from depression.

God's lifting hand often looks like the hands of real

people all around us.

The sign above my therapist's door stated, "This is going to hurt before it gets better." And it did. It hurt to delve into the dark places and learn coping skills that had eluded me so long. It hurt something awful, but not as awful, I told myself, as continuing on in despair. So I reached over the plaid couch, and over the silk flowers, and grabbed hands with the counselor; and I reached over phone lines and grasped hold of friends who never gave up on me when all I did was cry out loud; and I reached for my husband in the dark and clung to him.

If you are deep in the mire, and in desperate need of lifting, then tilt your head toward heaven and raise your hands for help. He brought me up out of the pit of destruction, out of the miry clay... He is strong enough to save, able to lift, and often does it through the flesh-and-blood people in our midst.

When a mess becomes our message...

> *"He...set my feet upon a rock making my footsteps firm. He put a new song in my mouth, a song of praise to our God; Many will see and fear and will trust in the LORD." Psalm 40:2-3*

I spent the first three sessions with the counselor just crying. I was embarrassed, most of all that I couldn't stop myself.

But she waited and nodded and kept extending her hand across the great divide. And when I was finally able to gulp down enough air to fill my broken lungs and exhale in a way that formed words, this is what I asked her: "I know where I'm going to end up on the other side of this, I just don't know how to get there. Won't you tell me what the next step is?"

She smiled hope and squeezed my hand, "No, I can't. All I know is that right now you're having a good cry. But you're right, you will get to the other side."

What she didn't say is that there on the other side is something more amazing than I ever imagined...Not only is it the complete, restored me standing there, it's my story, my testimony, my smile. It's the new song in my mouth. It's the hymn of praise to my God. And many are seeing me here, and have put their trust in the Lord.

Amazing!

I've heard it, how God takes our mess and makes it our message—how God takes our test and turns it on its ear, making it our testimony. But it's true. It's absolutely true! Press on; it's true!

I don't know what step you're on; Calling Out Loud, Grabbing Hold of Hands, Knee Deep in Tears, in the Process of Being Lifted, or standing with me on the Other Side,

Testifying to the One Who Saves...But the only part of the equation that is true for every one of us who believes is what's at the end of the journey: A New Song.

Depression isn't always a Spiritual Condition—But the Answer is Pure Spirit.

For those of you still in the mud, the muck, and the mire of depression with little ones all around, and you're exploding because your adrenal glands are shot and you feel like a hot mess each day, I want to tell you the hardest part of all for me. There was this tendency to feel like I was failing spiritually. "If only I was abiding, believing, and praying more...then I wouldn't be so downcast. Then I would bear the fruit of JOY!" But sometimes, there are medical, hormonal, neurological reasons so complex that our abiding selves still don't bear the fruit of God's Spirit this side of glory.

Why?

I could say, "I don't know," and that'd be the truth, but I think I might. I think God lets His holy people experience great soul depression so that they learn the passionate, saving love that raises us to life again, the redeeming love that sets us on a firm foundation, that puts a new song in our mouths and becomes the anthem inspiring faith from those who have not yet heard.

I believe that the Spirit of God is mighty at work in the midst of a Christian mom's depression.

I used to think that the happy life was the life blessed by God. But here I am, after taking all the steps I didn't know how to take there in the therapist's office, and I see that the blessed life is the life that had to CRY OUT; the blessed life is the life that had to GRAB HOLD HARD; the blessed life was cultivated in the persevering faith of a hurting heart; the blessed life experienced the LIFTING; and the blessed life now TESTIFIES TO THE SAVING.

Ask me why I smile. I dare you to ask this broken woman who used to explode into a million fragmented pieces at home in front of her children, whom God has built back up and made whole again, why she smiles in the grocery store, in the pick-up line at her children's school, coming out of Sunday morning worship...Ask her why she smiles, ask her why she sings.

LET'S PRAY:

"Dear Lord, I am deep in the mud, in the muck, and the mire, and in desperate need of lifting. My heart gets so sad sometimes. Though I have all the blessings in the world, still I feel stuck. Would You please, Lord, take me by the hand and lead me out of the dark and into the light of Your presence.

Give me the eyes to see, the ears to hear, and the mind to perceive Your good plan each step of the way. You are my refuge and my strength, and I run into You, amen"

Wendy

CHAPTER 19: EXHAUSTION

I was prepared, as usual. When my firstborn son came into the picture, I was large and in charge of everything in my life. I'm a type-A, super organized overachiever with a Master's Degree in Leadership and Educational Administration. I taught teenagers for 10 years and never felt like I was facing a personality or obstacle that could undo me and my "can-do" attitude. As my due date with my firstborn arrived, I was certain that this motherhood thing was going to go smoothly and according to my plans.

And then Oliver was born with severe reflux and colic that lasted well beyond his first year of life. This capable woman had suddenly become capable of just about nothing in the baby department.

Oliver didn't sleep through the night until he was 3 years old. We tried everything under the sun to get him to feel better and train him to sleep. My husband Guy and I spent the first 18 months of Oliver's life swaddling, rocking, consoling, and feeding him just so he wouldn't scream at top volume All. Night. Long.

Sleep experts gave us our money back.

Chiropractors threw their hands in the air.

Friends had no magic formulas, though we tried them all.

I will never forget the mind-numbing depression of my fatigue during our baby's infancy and beyond.

Eventually, I heard God whisper to my heart that *He would hold me while I held Oliver*, all through the night. Hour after hour. Day after day. I CHOSE to love him in my extreme weariness.

As if the nights were not long enough, Ollie only napped for 15 minutes at a time, so the stalwart determination to nurture him through this nightmarish chapter of our lives had to be supernatural. I could barely function. My husband and I *simply existed* during this time in our lives, but we finally came to a place of peace where we accepted that we were bone tired, drained, and physically and mentally empty.

We knew that we couldn't *fix* it.

Finally, we realized that loving one another and our precious boy through our weariness was a refining test that God was walking us through as a family. It meant being patient when we felt on edge, speaking kindly when we wanted to lash out, and yielding our will to God's.

I couldn't change my son. God had to change *me*.

When we are tired, we must dig deeper, speak slower, think more carefully, and move about more gently than ever before, because we are so much more prone to lash out in our weariness. Because we have the Holy Spirit in our lives, there is NOTHING we cannot do in Christ: "I can do all this through Him who gives me strength." (Philippians 4:13, NIV)

Maybe you don't have a newborn at this chapter of your life, but sometimes, it's our kids' behavior that makes us weary. They seem to never "get it," and we feel like a broken record. In those tiresome moments, weeks, months, or years, here is my mantra:

> *"So let's not get tired of doing what is good. At just the right time we will reap a harvest of blessing if we don't give up." (Galatians 6:9, NLT)*

Moms, we all need to remember that the race we are running is not easy. That's okay! God wants us to do good works as evidence of our faith, and to know that we will "reap a harvest if we do not give up." Let's not give in to the lie we tell ourselves that we just can't do it one more hour, or one more day. That's the very moment we yield to the Lord and say, "Father, I don't have strength in myself. Please revive me!"

I had to succumb to the fact that I couldn't change the circumstances that were making me weary, before I could ask God to give me hope and joy in the midst of my frustrations.

Take a seat in that rocking chair and settle in for the opportunity to pray over your kids, your neighbors, and your country when you rise the umpteenth time in the night to console your baby, instead of erupting in anger or sinking in helplessness.

Sit down on the floor when your toddler hits his little sister— again—and lovingly but firmly take his hands in yours instead of shouting at him in anger or backhanding him.

Recall to mind the words and actions that your son's specialist has prescribed for you as you deal with his specific medical condition or behavioral challenge and choose to have hope. Consider this "your thing," and determine to serve his many needs with joy as an act of loving sacrifice to your Savior Who chose you to be his mom.

Choose to be as joyful and purposeful in your words, tone, actions, and motivation at 5:00 PM as you are at 5:00 AM.

Go ahead and train your kids to speak to one another with

respect, again and again, instead of giving up on them in the midst of their sibling rivalry. Are you exhausted and is it exhausting? Yes and yes.

I couldn't change my circumstances during that first year of motherhood. Even now, I deal with long-term behavior issues in each of my kids. But as long as they are in my home, my job is to not give in to my exhaustion or weariness from parenting them.

Every challenging moment with my child can be a victory for ME, even if it is not for THEM. There can always be a victor in our toughest and most draining moments. That is the biblical response that I want to focus on today.

••••••••••••••••••••••••••••••••••

EVERY CHALLENGING MOMENT WITH MY CHILD CAN BE A VICTORY FOR ME, EVEN IF IT IS NOT FOR THEM.

••••••••••••••••••••••••••••••••••

Will you "dig deep" today with me, through Christ? Can we give each other a virtual pep talk come 2:00 or 6:15 or in the predawn hours, reminding one another to finish well in the strength of the Holy Spirit?

To this day, I still have one son who wakes often in the night. I haven't had more than six consecutive hours of sleep for many years. We may not get the refreshing or reviving we need to feel 100% each day, but that has no real bearing on our ability to respond biblically in the hard moments that will come our way. **Be exhausted if you must, but give your kids your best self anyway.**

And remember that in "due time," "we will reap a harvest if we do not give up."

LET'S PRAY:

"Lord! I'm exhausted. Weary. So very tired. I need Your strength to make it through today. I know that You want me to persevere. I don't want to give up, Lord, so help me to press on, knowing this is only a chapter of my life and not forever. Help me to rely on You when I am mentally, emotionally, and spiritually weak. Allow me to be willing to endure every hardship as a way to yield my will to Yours. I don't want to take out my exhaustion on my children by being short-tempered. Jesus, you also grew bone-tired when You were on earth as a human being. You understand the way I feel. Thank You for being willing to suffer for my sake and for being a God Who sees me. I put my hope in You and trust You for the harvest to come at the proper time. In Your name I pray, amen!"

Amber

CHAPTER 20: RUNNING LATE

• •

I have a friend named Angie who is love, joy, and patience personified. She is my peer, but she is also my Titus 2 example of how to gently and faithfully care for my family. I often say that when I grow up, I want to be just like Angie! And when my children tell me I'm the best mom in the whole wide world, I smile and say, "Second best... don't forget Ms. Angie." And we all have a good laugh together, because it's true—of course, my children promise that they'd rather have me anyway! And when we go to Disneyland I tell them that we're at "The Happiest Place on Earth!" But my middle child slides up close and says, "I like Ms. Angie's house better."

Ms. Angie is my flesh-and-blood example of the mom I want to be.

One day we were chatting at her kitchen island, over a cup of tea, as the children played in the backyard. (By the way, the kids were jumping on the trampoline, battling each other with Nerf swords, while the only girl at the little party sprayed them with a hose! So you see why this is better than Disneyland.)

Anyway, Angie was smiling and serving and encouraging,

and doing everything she does so naturally, when I brought up my most recent mom-fail. I had been short tempered with my oldest son earlier that day. Angie was quick to remind me that we all have bad mothering moments, that we're not perfect, that we can learn from our failures, ask for forgiveness, and do better next time. I was shocked to hear her lump herself in with the rest of us when she said these next words...

"When I haven't gotten enough sleep or we're running late somewhere...that's when I blow it."

Ladies, even the most gentle of souls can lose their footing when they're tired and running late. And goodness, don't those two things absolutely describe the early years of motherhood? It's like ascending a rocky mountain with only a few hours of interrupted rest, and half an hour late! But you need all your faculties to climb safely to the precipice. A tired hiker is a dangerous hiker. And if you're running late, you're likely to slip and fall.

Parenting is like climbing Mt. Everest over and over, each and every day, with our children in tow! It's a mammoth climb, and a holy ascent as we lead them upward! Leading them to the high places; up to the mountain where our help comes from.

A Song of Ascents.

I will lift up my eyes to the mountains;
From where shall my help come?
My help comes from the Lord,

Who made heaven and earth.
He will not allow your foot to slip.
(Psalm 121:1-3, NIV)

When we are running late, rushed, and ruffled… falling and failing comes fast and furious. But falling and failing can't become the norm, because God has called us to ascend His hill with clean hands and a pure heart, not lifting up our souls to falsehood or swearing deceitfully (Psalm 24:3-4), and definitely not blowing it with our kids each time we're running late again. He's called us to climb each mountainous day righteously! His desire is that we walk the challenging path before us, side by side with our children, with integrity by the help of His Holy Spirit. So He gives us His strength when we are weak, and sure feet when we are running late upon the craggy ledges.

> *"The Sovereign LORD is my strength; he makes my feet like the feet of a deer, he enables me to tread on the heights." (Habakkuk 3:19, NIV)*

Three practical things to do each day when tardiness is your trigger.

Put yourself to bed!

I know that the temptation is to suck those quiet hours dry late at night, but if you don't sleep, then you'll be bone dry come morning. This is foundational. Get good sleep, moms and dads: you need to be ready and rested for each new tomorrow. Get to bed, and don't forget to set your alarms for an early date with the Lord when you are fresh and refreshed —in your quiet time together, He will prepare you for the mountainous day ahead.

Prepare

Preparing for your busy day is important. Few people can just swing it and stay calm when there are children climbing by your side. One of the ways I prepare is by laying out clothes and packing lunches on school nights. I prepare by keeping a running grocery list so that I can make one orderly trip to the store rather than multiple frenzied trips each day. Keeping a calendar helps me to be prepared, too. Communication also plays a key role. I feel more prepared for each day's ascent when I've talked it through with my husband.

Plan

"Planning" is a word I keep coming back to in my own climbing, mothering life. Not only do I plan and prepare for my priorities, I also plan out what I should say and do when my plans aren't working out. I have to know what I should say and how I should say it when every one of my children is meandering to the car when we are pressed for time; when the children cry over baths and it's an hour past bedtime; when we've been invited to a friend's house for dinner, but my kids haven't picked up the driveway and I'm stuck waiting for one billion balls and bicycles to be moved out of the way before I can peel out of the driveway with a scowl on my face!

Plan right words when their behavior is wrong... so that your behavior remains right.

And plan in plenty of margin, too. Margin is the white space that surrounds the words in a book. Margin is the padding in your bank account so that you're not riding the bottom of your resources. Margin is planning to be at church 15 minutes early, so there's no stress when you're running 15 minutes late. Margin is low-stress Saturday mornings and Friday night movie nights at home. Margin takes planning.

PLAN RIGHT WORDS WHEN THEIR BEHAVIOR IS WRONG... SO THAT YOUR BEHAVIOR REMAINS RIGHT.

How can you make a new plan to ascend each day on time? Are there simple, practical things you can do to be ready? Does it require waking up earlier? Keeping shoes by the door? Putting up a cork board so you aren't losing all your important papers and dates? Maybe it does. However, maybe the main reason you're always late is because of the children. Especially that one child who can't transition from play time to grabbing his shoes and moving out the door. Maybe his lethargy and lack of hurry make you want to scream, "For crying out loud!" But you can't do that…so you need a plan.

Here's a suggestion: Look him in his eyes, take him by the hand, and walk him to his shoes when he's struggling to move in a timely manner. You'll be able to do this without anger if you've factored in that margin. Of course, when we're tired and running late…we simply can't manage to help him, so we holler. And we think his slowness is our trigger. But maybe it's not. Maybe our lack of margin is the real culprit.

How does this apply to your life? Where do you need to pad in more margin so that you're not always running late in the course of each new day? Grace lives in those extra moments. Those extra moments allow us to help the child who's lost her toothbrush and the one who can't find his shoes and the one who you just found under his covers again.

"The Lord passed before him and proclaimed, 'The Lord,

the Lord, a God merciful and gracious, slow to anger, and abounding in steadfast love and faithfulness.'" (Exodus 34:6)

There's no time in your busy life for this slow-to-anger sort of parenting unless we put ourselves to bed, prepare for each new day's climb, and plan for margin on the mountain.

LET'S PRAY:

"Dear Lord, give me Your strength when I am weak and Your patience when we are running late. Give me Your peace and Your perspective on what really matters when we are hurried throughout long days together. I want You, Lord, Your Presence to lead me up the mountain—as I lead my children. Yes, that's my prayer today. In Jesus' name, amen."

Wendy

CHAPTER 21: NO PERSONAL SPACE

··

I had had enough. As a mom of three boys, I was used to the fact that I lived in a "Testoster-HOME" of deafening noise, stinky odors, and mud-tracked floors. But when the ball flew through the air and hit me in the head, it was the last straw! I had already been stepped on, pushed, and accidentally run over by a skateboard, all in the span of an hour.

"NO MORE!" I roared.

Everyone froze.

All three of my boys stood looking at me with eyes wide open in surprise. They were used to their mom being tough, able to roll with the punches. Literally. My frustration overpowered their kinetic energy and they waited for me to continue.

Instead, I sat down on the floor in a heap and sighed heavily.

Some days, the physical demands and lack of personal space can get to me. I'm a girly-girl, and there is nothing I love more than a mani-pedi and high tea with friends. Instead, most days I am chasing Nerf gun darts and wrestling with my sons. Don't get me wrong, I love that! But, in my moment of weakness, it seemed to me that I had every right to have a pity party and demand an injury-free zone that encompassed a five-foot circumference around me.

I had similar moments when my kids were younger, too.

We moved to a small town several years ago, and I found myself without family and only a few friends. I was a stay-at-home mom of a four-year-old, an

THE TRUTH IS THAT WHEN I AM POURING MYSELF OUT FOR OTHERS, I AM BEING LIKE CHRIST.

almost two-year-old, and a newborn baby. My husband worked insane hours and I would go for days on end without ever getting out of my pajamas. My brain was turning to sludge and I felt like all I did on any given day was breastfeed and change diapers. *Repeat.* I had to carry one kid in a carrier on my back while I cradled the other in front and tried to keep an eye on the third running around the house. I felt like my body belonged to everyone but me.

As a mom with young and needy children, and now as a mom with older kids who often catch me in the crosshairs of their rough-and-tumble play, I can get to the point where I simply say, "Enough!" It would be very easy for me to crumble under a self-focused and defeatist outlook. But I don't have to.

Our attitudes are what we make them.

I don't really *have* to get angry. I don't really *have* to be quick to anger and lose my self-control. I don't really *have* to tell myself that I deserve to have peace and quiet. And I don't really *have* to give in to the temptation to think that in those harried moments, my life would be better if I could just have my own space.

The truth is that when I am pouring myself out for others, I am being like Christ.

He didn't have nice digs, fancy clothes, or an entourage of assistants. He lived simply, pouring Himself out for others, even to the point of great fatigue and distress. He did all of those things with you and me in mind. And He did it out of unconditional love.

In chapters 8 and 9 of the book of Matthew, we get a glimpse of Jesus' work ethic and attitude when others placed high demands on Him and infringed on His personal space. He went from town to town healing people, casting out demons, combating the Pharisees who judged His motives and power, and calming storms on the sea. He preached in the synagogues, taught the crowds, and spent time training his disciples. Even his meals were interrupted by those in need. The crowds pressed in around Him so closely that a sick woman reached out to touch His cloak and was healed. (Matthew 9:20)

Although Jesus often took time for Himself, on this particular day, it seemed He could never catch a break.

And He didn't.

After all those endless demands, Matthew 9:36 says, "When he saw the crowds, he had compassion on them, because they were harassed and helpless, like sheep without a shepherd." Jesus could very well have sat down with a heavy sigh and told everyone to go away. He too could have roared, "NO MORE," but He didn't. He had compassion.

Jesus understands our weaknesses. The Bible tells us in Hebrews 4 that Jesus experienced the same enticements we do when He walked on earth as God in human flesh, and yet He never sinned. The Message puts it like this:

> *"Now that we know what we have—Jesus, this great High Priest with ready access to God—let's not let it slip through our fingers. We don't have a priest who is out of touch with our reality. He's been through weakness and testing, experienced it all—all but the sin. So let's walk right up to him and get what he is so ready to give. Take*

the mercy, accept the help." (Hebrews 4:14-16, MSG)

Jesus sympathizes with us when we would rather have a mud bath at a spa than wipe dirt from our floors. He knows what it feels like to have temptation breathing down our necks. That's what makes Him so willing and able to extend mercy to us in our times of weakness. He is ready to help us when we ask.

I'm not saying that moms can't take care of themselves or that we should feel guilty for taking breaks away from kids or having date nights with our spouses. Those are good things that we need to do and should do. But I'm wondering if you, like me, have room for growth in the attitude and perspective department. The Christian life is the servant life.

It's not a life where personal space rules; it's a life where pouring out ourselves for others reigns.

When my four-year-old thinks he's my third leg and I can't take two steps in front of me without tripping over him, I can treat him with compassion. He wants to be near ME! That's a gift! I don't need to think of it as an annoyance, do I?

When my boys are running past me with no regard for me and they elbow me in their haste, I can respond biblically, right? I can calmly, but firmly, say, "Hey, boys! I love that you have so much energy and I want you to have fun. But I also want you to be considerate of others. Ladies don't like to be elbowed. At least this one sure doesn't! Please take your game outside." I don't have to scream in frustration or sigh in annoyance. I can respond biblically with compassion and gentleness.

If I see a need, I can set aside time to train my kids with a loving attitude so they understand my expectations, and I can be patient with them as they learn, can't I?

And at the end of the day, even if my children still don't understand my needs for personal space, my example is to persevere, believing that I have a loving Father who is familiar with all my ways and waits to give me both grace and strength to do it again the next day.

Jesus left His throne of perfection to dwell among mankind and give up all His rights for my sake and for yours. Surely, we can alter our perspectives as mothers and extend a portion of that kind of sacrifice in our own homes. Let's welcome our kids into our personal space and be a reflection of our very personal Lord and Savior.

LET'S PRAY:

"Dear Jesus, Your example to us is one of selflessness and total humility. Out of compassion, You extended Yourself to incorporate the needs of others. You treated others as You

would want to be treated, often at Your own expense for personal comfort. I know that we need to take care of ourselves, but I don't need to react with anger or frustration when my own needs are not being met. Lord, help me to be more like You! Search my heart and see if there is any selfishness in me and replace it with humility. Allow Your Holy Spirit to change my need for more personal space with a willingness to lay down my life for the sake of my children. Accept this as an act of worship, Jesus—a sacrifice of praise to You! In Your Name, amen!"

Amber

CHAPTER 22: GOING IT ALL ALONE

Sometimes my husband's work week starts before the Sabbath sun has set. Leaving for the airport straight from church, leaving me to parent alone for the better part of another week—week after week. Others of you have husbands who are always there, but not present. They sit on the couch as you bathe every child and make the rounds, tucking children in. They leave their plates on the table, expecting you to clear it all, expecting you to usher the children into the bathroom to brush their teeth and wash their hands, then load them into the car for preschool, and come home to finish breakfast dishes. And then there are a great many of you who are single moms, doing it, quite literally, all alone. This chapter is for all of us.

My mom was a single mom. My parents divorced before I was three. I was a latchkey kid, coming home to an empty house, snacking on canned Betty Crocker Vanilla Frosting, a few too many gummy vitamins, and a bottle of soda. My brother and I spent the night at my dad's house every other weekend and every Wednesday night. And life became routine that way.

Routine.

WHEN THE WORLD FEELS LIKE IT'S SPINNING OFF ITS AXIS, ROUTINE PUTS A LITTLE ORDER BACK IN OUR ORBIT.

I can't help but breathe a sigh of relief when I think of that word. In the chaos of going it alone, routine gives order to our days and predictability to our struggles. Routine says, "I know he will be home on Friday night!" or "I know that Bible study is Thursday, and those women are always so kind to pray for me." Routine is getting out the door by 7am, and coming home with the crock-pot simmering on Mondays and a bag of Chick-fil-A in your hand on Tuesdays, and Grandma coming over to make pancakes on Saturday mornings. Routine is Sunday night trips for Froyo, and singing the same song over your children each and every night. Routine.

Routine helps both moms who are doing it on their own, and children who are missing a near and present dad. **When the world feels like it's spinning off its axis, routine puts a little order back in our orbit.** Routine can stop us from reeling.

That's a nice little pearl to put in your pocket for the day-in-day-out grind, when there's no one there to lend a hand with homework or bills. But what about those times you need a partner to soothe your loneliness? How about the times your teenage son needs a father speaking words of life into his young, masculine heart? And what of the little girl who is desperate for a near-and-dear daddy, telling her she is beautiful and chosen? Routine may help when it's time to get dinner on the table and laundry all put away, but what of the deeper heart needs that don't get filled, because Dad's not there to fill them?

"Therefore, since we are surrounded by so great a cloud of witnesses, let us also lay aside every weight, and sin which clings so closely, and let us run with endurance the race that is set before us, looking to Jesus, the founder and perfecter of our faith, who for the joy that was set before him endured the cross, despising the shame, and is seated at the right hand of the throne of God." (Hebrews 12:1-2)

Here are three helpful, hope-filled applications you can take from Hebrews 12:1-2, when parenting falls solely on your shoulders.

1. Surround yourself and your children with a cloud of witnesses. This may be a couple of good family friends, where the parents are either married or single. This includes your children's youth program at church and your Bible study with friends. Hopefully you have grandparents and aunts and uncles who are close enough in proximity to fill some of the heart holes and practical needs as well.

2. Lay aside your sin. I know you can be short tempered and grouchy because everything is yours to carry; you can go to places of bitterness and resentment whether you're divorced or married and feeling abandoned. Sometimes the weight of it all can slip from your fingers and land painfully on their little feet. You feel angry and the anger slips out of you at the wrong person at the wrong time. Might I suggest that you purposefully and prayerfully lay it down in safe ways at safe times, so that you don't drop that load on anyone else? God tells us clearly that we are to shake off the shackles that keep us prisoners of sin and hold us back from righteousness. Lay it aside.

3. Run to Jesus—He is the Prize! I know you are running everywhere, as you parent without a partner, but let's not let the busyness of life interfere with the ultimate prize. Don't be detoured by daily distractions; keep your eyes fixed on Jesus! He is the prize! Jesus is the prize! He isn't just the perfecter of faith for the sake of our salvation. He is the prize for our lives today, in the middle of every struggle. **Jesus perfectly fits every hole left by every parent, left by every partner.**

Though my parents were divorced, my dad was not absent. He was very present in our lives on a weekly basis. We vacationed with him, he came to all our games, and he took us to church and sent us to camp. His presence was a purposeful part of our (broken) family routine. Still, by the very nature of divorce, he wasn't there all the time and holes were created in my young, developing heart. While it's taken me a couple dozen years to gain this wisdom, I see now that God used the deficits created from divorce as reservoirs to fill me up with Himself! People often ask me today why my faith is what it is, and I can honestly testify that I needed Jesus too much to make me whole and fill me up. And once He made me whole, I could not ever imagine life without Him and His faithful Spirit's continual filling.

Did God have a perfect plan when He created husband and wife, children and family? Yes, I believe that He did. But sin…

Still, Jesus is the great redeemer! Even in the midst of broken family life, Jesus is there working all things together for our good and His great glory. He rushes in and fills our deep holes, in order to make us whole. Our redemption started on the cross, and continues with every cross we bear.

If parenting alone is your reality, your cross, your trigger, I pray that you have an overwhelming sense of God's faithful nearness in this season. And as you grow to find joy in His presence, I trust that your children (His children) are watching and learning to depend upon their Heavenly Father, too. May those deficits they incur become reservoirs that hold an eternal measure of living water.

LET'S PRAY:

"Dear Lord, Your faithfulness to redeem and repair all of the hurting places in my life never ceases to amaze me. I ask, Father, that You grow in me a hunger for even more of You. I want to turn to You proactively in every wanting, weak, and worn-out place in my life. Fill me with Your faithful nearness that I might overflow blessings and joy into the lives of my little ones, rather than overflow fear and exhaustion. Fill me Lord, that I might be a fountain of Your Living Water. I ask this in Jesus' redeeming name, amen."

Wendy

CHAPTER 23: CHALLENGING RELATIONSHIPS WITH IN-LAWS AND LACK OF FAMILY SUPPORT

Years ago, I taught my high school English students Robert Frost's poem, "Mending Wall." One famous line from this poem is that "Good fences make good neighbors."⁵ Most of us realize that healthy boundaries in relationships are often necessary—there's a reason that sage Benjamin Franklin said that "Guests, like fish, begin to smell after three days." Few relationships are harder to apply boundaries to than those with our in-laws, and for good reason.

Our parents spend decades raising us, shaping us, guiding us. It can be hard for them to release us to our spouses, necessary as it is. Some in-laws simply don't understand how much they can either foster a healthy and supportive relationship for their child's marriage, or bring great division and harm to the union. The stress and pressure of poor relationships with our mother or fathers-in-law can cause frustration, anger, and bitterness, which can easily infect our marriages, and, therefore, our children. And sometimes it's our brother or sisters-in-law that can do just as much good or harm.

How are we supposed to navigate these complex relationships, and how do we avoid the volatile triggers they can create?

When I met my wonderful and godly mother-in-law for the first time, I knew that she wasn't going to play the kind of role I had always dreamed of. Years before I met her, she suffered several major strokes and was wheelchair bound, living in a home for the elderly and disabled. I knew that my husband and I would serve more like parents to her than the other way around.

But my husband also had older siblings who were more like parents to him, and so in some ways, I suddenly had four sets of protective in-laws to navigate. Their family was a close-knit bunch of loyal Italians, and they have been generous and kind to us over the years. I had difficulty fitting in at first, though. In addition, my own family members had few boundaries in place, wanting to be involved in our lives a little too much.

My husband Guy and I realized early on that we needed to become a strong new unit as a couple and that we could both firmly, yet lovingly, set boundaries with our in-laws on BOTH sides. That's never easy. Many of the couples who have shared with me over the years have varying issues, from overly intrusive parents, to disregarding their parenting styles and requests, to extreme favoritism over their son or daughter as opposed to their new in-law.

If we choose to respond biblically, I believe that most cases can result in peace and unity in our families, even if it still hurts at times.

Here are 4 things to consider when navigating these important relationships:

1. As spouses, we must communicate, listen, and be united as a couple about the problem with our in-laws, and choose to protect our marriages above all else.

If your spouse is suffering or struggling as a result of conflict with extended family members, that should be your main priority. God instructs us to "leave" the home and authority of our parents and "cleave" to the new relationship we are building with our spouses. If your husband is not standing with you in solidarity over any particular issue, or vice versa, then the first matter of business is to work on your marriage —which may very well necessitate biblical counseling.

Ultimately, if we feel secure and safe in our marriage and our spouse's commitment to preserve our relationship and unique family goals and beliefs, then the anxiety over pressure from in-laws is greatly reduced. Sometimes, that means being grateful for your spouse and the new life you get to create together, instead of wasting time lamenting the dream of having ideal in-laws. Let go of the things you simply can't change.

2. Ask yourself if *your part* in the equation looks like this:

"Let no corrupting talk come out of your mouths, but only such as is good for building up, as fits the occasion, that it may give grace to those who hear. And do not grieve the Holy Spirit of God, by whom you were sealed for the day of redemption. Let all bitterness and wrath and anger and clamor and slander be put away from you, along with all malice. Be kind to one another, tenderhearted, forgiving one another, as God in Christ forgave you." (Ephesians 4:29-32)

Offer the same respect, honor, and godly treatment of our in-laws as we are commanded to demonstrate to all people, regardless of how they treat us or our children. If you have sin in your own life in this area, it's time to work on your part first.

3. I like to take the confusion of making choices as a parent out of the equation by following this one cardinal rule:

NEVER MAKE DECISIONS BASED ON FEARS OR BECAUSE OF PEERS.

Never make decisions based on FEARS or because of

PEERS.

This applies to our in-laws, too. Sometimes, moms over-discipline or give in to requests they don't feel comfortable with when they are with extended family. We have to become very self-aware and confident in our own decisions so that we don't behave towards our children or in-laws as a result of fear or peer pressure.

If this is a struggle for you, prepare yourself before you meet with them so that you have a clear image in mind of how you will behave as the wife and mom in your family, and do not give in to fear or pressure. God gave you authority over your home and children, and honoring how the Lord leads you is what matters most. Be authentically you, and if they don't accept that, it's okay. That rejection may require some grieving on our part, but this too is an opportunity to draw near to God. He accepts us just as we are, and following His leading is what will bring us peace, not the approval of our in-laws.

4. Just as Wendy and I have talked a lot about being consistent, planning out our right responses beforehand, and training our children intentionally with loving-kindness, we can take a lot of the fight out of our in-law relationships in much the same way.

When my child persists over an issue and I have already

communicated clearly with him, I don't have to get angry, upset, or continue to argue with him. I can simply say something like, "Son, I understand that you want to stay up late, but as your mom I know that you need sleep and it's now bedtime. Please go into the bathroom to brush your teeth and I will help you get dressed for bed. Would you like to wear your Star Wars pajamas or your Captain America ones?" They may whine and complain. And again, we can empathize and repeat our same statement of expectation, following through on our standard.

When in-laws become emotional, manipulative, or threaten our boundaries, we can respond in a similar fashion to them as we do to our wayward kids. We can calmly and kindly say to Grandma and Grandpa, "I appreciate that you want to spoil our kids with sugary treats because you are loving grandparents, but John and I know that their bodies can't handle it. We can provide snacks for you to give them that are healthy but still yummy, or we can give you a list of ones we recommend if you want to shop for them yourself. Just let us know which you prefer." If they dishonor your repeated request, then you may need to follow up by explaining that the kids simply won't be eating at their house. You don't need to become embroiled in an argument or crumple under manipulation.

Eventually, it may be necessary to explain that, if they simply don't respect your decisions, you may have to come up with some creative alternatives—just as we do with our children when they don't honor our role. It may mean that you need to take some time away from the relationship altogether, or put some more secure boundaries in place, but this should always be lovingly and clearly communicated, not an act of bitter punishment or unhealthy division.

The Bible puts it like this in Romans 12:17-18: "Do not repay anyone evil for evil. Be careful to do what is right in the eyes of everyone. If it is possible, as far as it depends on you, live at peace with everyone."

As wives, we can either add pressure to our husband's burden or we can cultivate peace with both sets of in-laws. I love this verse from Proverbs 12:16: "The vexation of a fool is known at once, but the prudent ignores an insult." Sometimes, we go into get-togethers with family with a bee in our bonnet. We are easily vexed because we anticipate we will be. And it may very well be true that some in-laws seem intent on hurting us. "But the prudent ignores an insult," doesn't she? Never underestimate the power of prayer and your own gracious spirit towards your spouse, your children, and other relatives. Expect the Lord to prepare their hearts as much as yours, and ask God to give you wisdom. In-law relationships may very well be the biggest challenge you will face in your marriage, but they don't have to leave you in turmoil that negatively affects your kids. Keep doing the good parenting, entrust your commitment as a family to the

Lord, and walk in faith that God will honor your desire for peace.

I'm not sure if my own in-law relationships on either side of my family will ever be what I dreamed of, but that's okay. I choose to be grateful for the many ways that they have helped shape me and my husband. Seeking peace and pursuing it is the mark of a daughter of the King of Kings; pleasing Him by our godly responses to any conflict is the righteous thing to do and leads to blessing. When your mothers- or fathers-in-law can't be pleased, focus instead on pleasing your Heavenly Father, and you'll never be disappointed.

LET'S PRAY:

"Dear God, You ask us to be kind to everyone. Some people, like my in-laws, can be especially challenging to show kindness to. And yet, Lord, I know that we all have our rough edges, myself included. Lord, I want to do the right thing that honors You in all of my relationships. Bring peace to our family and help us all to be thoughtful, sensitive, and

gracious. I want to show respect because it's the right thing to do and I can never go wrong by doing what is right. Father, help me to feel genuine compassion and love for my family members, even if circumstances never change or personalities rub me the wrong way. Help me to be wise in setting healthy boundaries, but to always be ready to bless others when it is in my power to do so. Thank You! In Jesus' name, amen!"

Amber

CHAPTER 24: ALL THE NOISE!

Just the other day, I snapped a picture of my eldest son in our living room, his long man-legs propped up. It was a quiet moment as he read on the orange couch. An enormous white wall stood like a backdrop behind him, showcasing simple, clean lines. It was a peaceful picture of a peaceful moment. And as I looked at the picture later that afternoon, I was reminded again how much I love white space. I've thought a thousand times over about decorating that wall, but I'm just so in love with the blank walls.

Walls without tons of color and countertops without tons of clutter. All that white space feels calming and kind to my nerves in a home full of rough-and-tumble sons rolling pell-mell out of bed and straight into conflict and loud, happy sounds each day. So much noise. **Noise and boys and noisy boys assail my sensibilities from Son up to Son down.** But maybe you have squealing and giggling girls and always talking, always squawking...always girls! Either way, boys or girls, or a blessed mix of the two, it is easy to get overwhelmed the constant sounds of children.

Do you know what all that empty space over my couch says about me? **I need a lot of quiet to feel calm and collected,**

and without it I'm not so calm and not so collected. Quiet lovely moments are a lot like white space... but there isn't much of that these days. And my ears feel like they're going to bleed some afternoons, and I get all twitchy and out of sorts.

Which is why all the noise feels like stress on each and every one of my nerves. Because I experience peace in the empty spaces. I always have—I can see that looking back now. How I couldn't have a roommate in college because I needed long stretches of quiet rest. But that's not possible today, because these little roommates are my children! Though I function best in the quiet, and love clutter-free places...I'm a mom. What I want, and maybe even desperately need during this long mothering season, may not be possible.

So I must learn to behave myself, even when I don't get what I need! And then, at the same time, I must learn to carve out quiet so that I can get what I need. You see where I'm going here? There are two parts to this trigger tendency. **We must learn to cope by carving out the quiet, and learn to cope when there's no quiet to be found.** If the kids are loud and you've not had a moment's peace, you still have to remain kind and in control of yourself. Though it's your trigger, you aren't allowed to pull it back and wound those around you. You must learn to control yourself, even on the noisiest days.

A friend once told me, "My two boys don't have a volume

control, even though I have spoken to them about indoor and outdoor voices. All they have is happy-loud and angry-loud settings, but no soft indoor voice option. There have been times when I have blown up at them over the constant noise! When that happens, I ask God for His peace, and the relief is almost always instantaneous. The problem is remembering to ask *before* I become as loud as they are."

How about we learn to do the same? Let's not wait until we're exploding all over those white walls, all over our little people. Let's carve out calm and quiet moments to call upon the Lord.

Call on Him in the early morning hours, call on Him at noontime too, and call on Him throughout the long and loud evenings.

WE MUST LEARN TO COPE BY CARVING OUT THE QUIET, AND LEARN TO COPE WHEN THERE'S NO QUIET TO BE FOUND.

Pray Pray Pray...

I'm sure there are hundreds of blog posts and books, compiled by hundreds of moms, encouraging us where to go to refresh in sweet quiet, so as to cope with all the childish noise that tends to flip our triggers. But today, I'm curious what God's Word would have me do when I can't pull away. Though we admonish one another to get away and find some peace, today I want to know where His Word would send me to find it. What Scriptures would best guide me through the labyrinth of LOUD? What passages can lead me past the constant rowdy soundtrack of my days in search of peace?

And so, if your trigger to feeling overwhelmed in this mothering life is the ceaseless noise there in your home and in your car, at Target, on the way to church, and everywhere you go when they come, too...When what you lack is quiet, causing you to explode, then let's consider together where God tells us our peace can be found..."For He Himself is our peace..." (Ephesians 2:14a)

In Him.

"Abide in Me, and I in you. As the branch cannot bear fruit of itself unless it abides in the vine, so neither can you unless you abide in Me." (John 15:4) The fruit that we desperately desire when we feel chaos pressing in through our ears, in through our feminine pores, from all the rambunctious raucous, is peace. "But the fruit of the Spirit is love, joy, peace, patience, kindness, goodness, faithfulness, gentleness, self-control." (Galatians 5:22-23)

In Him.

Abiding in Him is the only white space that can ever truly

still the quaking in our overwhelmed souls. Though a mani/ pedi sounds divine, God has promised, "Peace I leave with you; My peace I give to you; not as the world gives do I give to you." (John 14:27a) "I have told you these things, so that in me you may have peace. In this world you will have trouble. But take heart! I have overcome the world." (John 16:33, NIV)

In Him.

I'm stringing these verses together, believing they just might be the answer for some of us. For those of us who can't seem to cope with all the noise that just won't stop. And so instead of a list of where to go, let's consider together when to go.

In Him.

He is the peace in our days...the space when space is tight...the quiet over our quiver. During the crazy-making days raising boys who make noise, raising noisy boys; raising girls with their high-pitched squeals and giggling conversation and questions without end. We can find, in Him, all we need, every waking hour.

In the morning—come to Him.
Open up His Word—sanctified in Him.
Over your coffee—turn to Him.
Cuddling close during naps—speak of Him.

Over snacks—thanking Him.
Making dinner—praising Him.
Correcting loud conflicts—even then, with Him.

Oh, I pray this feels practical and not elusive, because He is real and ready to hold you when you start to shake within and without. And the more often you turn to Him before your explosive moments, the more His peace will become you so that those moments don't happen nearly so much. What I'm saying is...**Turn to Him so often that you end up looking at Him all the time! Glance at Him so much, you end up gazing at Him for the rest of your life.**

Remain all day "in Him"—and He will remain all day "in you" and you will bear His peace.

LET'S PRAY:

*"Dear Lord, You know the way You made me. You know how overwhelmed I can get with the constant noise. And You know that my heart's desire is to **learn to love them through the loud**. Refresh me with Your peaceful Spirit, and teach me when and where to pull away, that I might abide in You. For You are my peace, amen."*

Wendy

CHAPTER 25: ROUGHHOUSING

When my husband Guy and I were first married, we took a beautiful trip into the countryside to go apple picking. In the quaint little orchard town, we popped into a gift shop where they sold an array of children's items. To my surprise, my husband picked up a white newborn onesie that read "Princess" in pink and was embroidered with a tiara. He thought we should buy it for our future daughter, even though we weren't pregnant at the time.

Fast forward 10 years and 3 sons.

Our visions of sweet ballerinas coloring quietly in our playroom never came to fruition. Instead, we have a houseful of amazing and loud little boys who we wouldn't trade for the world, but with whom also come a different brand of triggers for an orderly mom like me. I'm a "place-for-everything-and-everything-in-its-place" kind of gal. But I have had to expand my definition of what home looks like: fewer china displays and more noisy train sets. And yes, roughhousing, too.

If you have a son, then most likely, you understand the need for both little dudes and big ones to amuse themselves by throwing each other around and displaying moves fit for a warrior. If you have more than one boy, then you understand that trying to contain roughhousing boys is like lassoing a tornado. As a tomboy girl, I relished horseplay with my older brother, so I know full well that rowdy behavior is not limited to "Testoster-HOMES". Thankfully, my boys have girl friends who can keep up with them in the roughhousing department.

Many moms have shared with me that roughhousing is one of their biggest anger triggers, and they wish they simply didn't have to deal with it. I totally get it. My first reactions to their clownery was to tell the circus in my living room to hit the road for the next town. But three boys later? Personally, I want my boys to roughhouse. I see their need for it and the way they somehow bond over wrestling one another to the ground. Biologically, their bodies crave activity and taking risks. It's the way God designed them! **Being a good steward of our sons means allowing them room to be boys. And loving our girls who are more disorderly than dainty is good stewardship, too.**

Their behavior isn't wrong, but my reactions to their cringe-worthy moves can be. The initial way to accommodate both their need for rough-and-tumble play and my desire for peace is to become a proactive mom who teaches them what is okay and what is not by setting reasonable boundaries. We can't let them go crazy, then get mad at them if we haven't set ground rules, or assume they know what drives us to frustration.

The best parenting occurs outside of conflict, and yet that is when we try to teach kids lessons—at the very moment when emotions are high and they are most resistant. We run into the room where we hear screeching and witness ninja-style moves, yelling at our kids to stop and giving them a lecture about unruly behavior in the heat of the moment. That rarely works! **We need to become proactive parents instead of reactionary ones.** When my kids are wound up tighter than a drum, running on adrenaline, or emotionally distraught, they are not going to be receptive to my training.

I can table the talk till their hearts unlock! If I find that I am trying to damage control day in and day out, then I'm

································
WE NEED TO BECOME PROACTIVE PARENTS INSTEAD OF REACTIONARY ONES.
································

probably attempting to teach my kids a lesson at the wrong time. Work "roughhouse" training into your agenda before the battles ever get underway in the first place. That's proactive parenting!

The thing that matters the most to God is that we love Him

and we love others, even when they have their brother pinned to the kitchen floor. I know that the desire to nip rough-housing in the bud with our own rough admonition is tempting, especially if they are truly disobeying us or ignoring a parameter we have previously set with them. But it's certainly not loving. The Biblical response to any situation that we feel is a personal bother or irritation is to humble ourselves and speak the Truth in love.

I Corinthians 13:3-7 from The Message reminds us:

> *If I give everything I own to the poor and even go to the stake to be burned as a martyr, but I don't love, I've gotten nowhere. So, no matter what I say, what I believe, and what I do, I'm bankrupt without love.*
> *Love never gives up.*
> *Love cares more for others than for self.*
> *Love doesn't want what it doesn't have.*
> *Love doesn't strut,*
> *Doesn't have a swelled head,*
> *Doesn't force itself on others,*
> *Isn't always "me first,"*
> *Doesn't fly off the handle,*
> *Doesn't keep score of the sins of others,*
> *Doesn't revel when others grovel,*
> *Takes pleasure in the flowering of truth,*
> *Puts up with anything,*
> *Trusts God always,*

Always looks for the best,
Never looks back,
But keeps going to the end.

We are always responsible for *our* reactions to our triggers. Can we remain calm, intervene, give everyone some space, and speak with loving authority in the middle of the chaos? YES. We can. We don't have to stand by, allowing tension to build inside, and then explode at our unruly kids. Love can find a way to set aside our own preferences for the good of others.

Here are a few practical tips to help your kids roughhouse safely.

1. Make "Pool Noodle Light Sabers." This is THE BEST. Buy a one-dollar pool noodle and cut it in half. Use duct tape and wrap the end so that it creates a "handle" and use cool stick-on jewels to bedazzle the saber or make "buttons." We also use stickers to put their names on their light sabers. I make a ton of these at once and then keep them on hand. Our rules? No hitting someone unarmed, and no hitting in the head. Other than that, they can go to town. They can have hours of fun without getting hurt!

2. If you can't beat them, join them. Facilitate their shenanigans instead of letting it happen spontaneously, so that you are prepared for it. I work roughhousing as an activity into our day—usually by calling out a war cry, boy-mom style, and engaging them in battle.

3. Setting healthy expectations doesn't have to make you a kill-joy! Again, be that proactive parent who teaches your kids in advance what appropriate roughhousing looks like in your home. Be UPBEAT during these conversations. This is meant to create safe FUN for everyone, not a doom and gloom "I'm-going-to-give-1,000-rules-and-ruin-your-fun" kind of conversation.

4. When "accidents" happen or bruises appear, don't panic. You don't have to swing into, "You are never roughhousing again!" mode. Obviously, I'm not talking about serious or dangerous injuries, but I let my kids get reasonably hurt and show them empathy, compassion, and love…usually as they run off to get right back to it. If I don't overreact (and look away a lot), we are all the better for it. My new mantra, as a mom of three boys and one dad who revel in the love language of roughhousing, is to "chill and go in the other room." Seriously.

5. Some friends like to roughhouse. Some don't. I can tell pretty quickly which homes/parks/friends are okay to mess around with/in and which ones aren't. So my boys know that when we are not at home, that if I say, "No roughhousing now." I mean it. That's when they simply need to yield to a different choice that I offer them for playtime. Again, we talk about this and practice it when it's not the heat of the moment so everyone is clear on expectations!

6. Create an alternative to actual wrestling or roughhousing. In our home we create what we call "a crash pile." I make a mountain of pillows, blankets, and other soft items in the living room and set up a designated chair they can jump off onto the crash pile. They know that they have to go one at a time and wait for the pile to clear before jumping, but this kind of structured chaos works for me!

Motherhood often looks a lot different from what we imagined. That's certainly true for me and my husband who traded princess tiaras for light sabers. I may not love the idea of roughhousing, but I love my children. I want them to see me taking it all in stride, sacrificing my desire for tranquility to nurture them in the things they need.

LET'S PRAY:

"Dear God, I know that my boys want to roughhouse and wrestle. You created their bodies to move and be active. I'm thankful that they have the energy to do so, but it can be hard for me to watch, let alone condone. Help me to be calm when the roughhousing and noise levels rise, and give me the right words to say to set safe guidelines. Lord, protect my kids and keep them safe! Remove the worry that I have for them and give me Your assurance that You are with us in the midst of

crazy fun chaos! I want to be a joyful mom, even during roughhousing. Thank You for stretching me out of my comfort zone and for helping me to speak with love, even when my nerves are frazzled! In Jesus Name, amen!"

Amber

CHAPTER 26: MESSY HOMES

•••

"Without oxen a stable stays clean, but you need a strong ox for a large harvest." (Proverbs 14:4, NIV)

Some of you married farmers. Most of us did not. Still, the imagery here is full of application for every mother in every messy home: You want a fruitful family? Then you're going to have a messy house! You want your little people and their friends and neighborhood kids all dropping by? You want to host home group with your church friends? You want children who have the freedom to finger paint at an easel and play in backyard dirt? Then you're going to have to deal with muddy shoes, sticky fingerprints, and careless spills.

You can wrap your mind around that concept, can't you? And yet, the reality feels overwhelming in your day-in and day-out lives as dishes and laundry pile up. Your husband is working out of town again this week, so the load falls squarely on your shoulders. You set a plan in place, how you're going to get it done after you tuck your children in bed for the night. All eleven loads of laundry are piled in a wrinkled mound upon your bed, and you have vowed to get every last piece of it folded and put away before you hit the sack! Except the youngest keeps coming out crying about "scary thoughts," and the oldest has leg cramps, and your husband texts, asking you to send him the phone number he scribbled on a scrap of paper three weeks ago that he's sure is on the back, right-hand corner of his desk. So you snap!

Messy homes are many women's triggers. And the problem is that as soon as we soothe our twitchy tendency by getting the place cleaned up, it's shot to pieces all over again—along with our nerves!

Does a messy home make a mess out of you?

Here's how it looks in our family: Our weekly routine is that the children all lend a hand and get their bedrooms and the family room picked up on Sunday nights, so that we're ready for a new week. Then it's off to bed and out the door in a hurry come morning. Needless to say, Monday is my happy, peaceful day. Except, within 18 seconds of getting home from school that afternoon, every Lego set we own, and every superhero ever made, carpets the floor once again. And...they're hungry! How DARE they be hungry when my stainless steal sink is so shiny and sparkly, without even a water spot? But in they come, like a herd of elephants, ripping through the pantry and grabbing granola bars, tearing off wrappers, sending pieces of their crumbly snack flying across the ground. And as I holler, "Grab a plate and eat that at the table..." another child pulls a juice box from the fridge, punches a hole in it with their straw, sending a sticky stream of kiwi-strawberry down the front of my cabinets...and I come undone. Again.

(insert screaming)

This is one of those triggers that I feel great shame over, because it's so predictable. I ought to have figured this out... conquered it by now. The confusing problem is, this isn't really about my house at all... my need for order in the home goes much deeper than a woman's affection for a freshly swept floor and Windex-ed windows. What I'm learning about my need for a clean home is that uncluttered countertops are a tangible way to rank the control I have over my life. When I can't control my husband's work schedule, my children's volume, their behavior at dinner or in their beds at night...I want to have just one aspect of my life in order. Just one. That's all I ask!

There are some mothers I know who struggle with eating disorders for the same over-arching reason, the hunger to control...something! So they overdo their exercise and under-do their calories. "If I can be a size 0... if I can not eat this whole day...if I can work out every day this week...then I won't feel so utterly out of control." But I digress...

"In his hand is the life of every living thing and the breath of all mankind." (Job 12:10)

Women, the application is simple. Hard, but simple. God is holding your every day in the expansive palm His hand. We are held in that hollow place beside every other thing under His sovereign control. The weight of eternity, the wars that rage around the globe, and our loved ones battling cancer. God is holding your life today, your family home today, your anxious heart today. **We can surrender big tears and big angst when we believe that a big God is in control.**

He is the one who has ordered your footsteps, His is the light that illuminates your path, His breath fills your being, and His Holy Spirit invites you

> **WE CAN SURRENDER BIG TEARS AND BIG ANGST WHEN WE BELIEVE THAT A BIG GOD IS IN CONTROL.**

to "be still and know" that He alone is God...even in the chaos.

Would your house be cleaner without your darling little mess makers? Would the wood floors stay shiny longer than the span of time it takes for them to dry? Would you only need to run the dishwasher (or the washing machine, for that matter) a time or two a week, rather than multiple times each day? Would your countertops and windows be free of peanut butter smudges and maple syrup fingerprints? Would you ever step again on a stray Lego in the middle of the night? Would your proverbial stable be so clean you could eat off of the floor?

Very likely.

The thing is, my dear friends with twitchy little trigger fingers, we don't have empty stalls. Our homes are full of strong little people with strong personalities, dirty socks, and toothpaste-crusted bathroom sinks.

The farmer and the mother are both keenly aware that the harvest can only be brought in from the fields with the help of strong animals. And God knew that much of our fruitful mothering lives happen in busy, bustling homes. Our children are part of the harvest themselves, our refinement is part of the harvest, and neighborhood and school friends may be part of the harvest as well, if we are willing to swing wide the stable doors. Embrace the harvest in your home, and thank God for the strong little creatures who are with you in the field each and every day.

It's all perspective!

LET'S PRAY:

"Dear Lord, You made this day and gave it to me as a gift. I don't want to control it and strangle the life-blood out of it. I

want to be a good steward of my moments, picking up and accomplishing what I can, but not at the expense of enjoying the gifts You've so generously bestowed upon me: The day itself, the breath in my lungs, my home, and the little oxen in my stalls, making a blessed mess out of it all again.

Give me a heart of thanksgiving, Lord, when complaints and bitterness seep in deep. Holy Spirit, slow me down and convict my heart before I run from room to room like a mad woman, blowing up at each and every person who dares cross my path, when I want things ordered and clean today. Help me to find peace within the chaos so that I don't explode like a toy chest after a cluttered day. And help me to see Your harvest in this messy stall season. Amen!"

Wendy

CHAPTER 27: THE PRESSURES OF MULTI-TASKING

I was a Junior in High School the first time I had a breakdown. Now, let me preface this by saying that I recognize "breakdown" is a really big (even clinical) term, and what I went through at sweet-sixteen may not seem overwhelming to anyone else. But my life had become the perfect storm to knock me off my young feet and sweep me out to sea, far from shore, with crushing waves. It was actually quite simple: I had taken on too much. I was going to a high school for performing artists in Downtown LA, I drove an hour each morning to get there, and stayed until late at night to rehearse a musical I was also doing at a local college. I wasn't getting enough sleep, I was missing my midweek youth group at church, and time with my family wasn't a priority.

By the end of the school year, I was in therapy, and my back was a tangle of muscles and nerves. My mom suggested I take the following semester off to return to my local high school just across the street from our suburban home. When you're overwhelmed, often times one small change radically changes it all. That next year, I walked across the street to school; even with extra-curricular theatre activities, I was home by 5pm each day. I made it to youth group every Wednesday night. The other evenings were spent with my family, finishing up homework, and getting a good night's rest. I started to heal both physically and emotionally.

A few years later, as a Sophomore in college, I got myself into a similar predicament. Too many classes, too many extras, too little sleep, too little godly fellowship. My back went out again, and I found myself in a fresh hot puddle of tears, this time on the other side of the country. I remember calling my mom and crying, "But I'm not taking on more than other students! I only have five classes and one play production. I'm not even working a part-time job! Why can't I do as much as everyone else?"

My mom's advice was clear and kind: "This has nothing to do with anyone else, we're talking only about you and what you can handle. If five classes are too many, then drop one."

"I feel like such a failure!" The words came fast and I remember the feel of them rolling off my tongue.

"A failure?" My mom asked. "Honey, a failure is the woman who doesn't recognize she's sinking. You are calling out for help and will make the changes necessary to succeed. That's not failure. That's success. And this lesson will lead you to succeed in other seasons of your life."

I hung up the phone and walked straight to the main admissions building to drop a class. Turns out, it was the last day of the semester to withdraw without penalty or charge, and there was a long line of young men and women waiting to do just that. I wasn't alone—not that it mattered (except it did). But even if I were the only one dropping a class that day…the lesson was simply that I had to find the load that I could handle.

To this day I can't handle multi-tasking well. It's part of my God-design.

However, I learned that when I cut back on all the multiple projects I'm "tasking" at once, I'm really quite good at this life God's giving me. As a matter of fact, I'm excited to tell you that I got straight A's that semester! Without too much on my plate, I was able to excel at my priorities. This is still true of me to this day: **When it comes to multitasking, I'm exceptional at a few things—but fail at many. Therefore, I must learn to build protective hedges around the most important people and responsibilities in my life.**

Trouble is, we can't "drop" one of our kids the way we can a college course. Instead, we need to learn to drop what we're doing, slow down, and assess what's on our plate and consider what might need to come off for the time being. It might be a leadership role for your church's MOPS group this year. Or hosting all of your family this holiday season.

Maybe helping in the Nursery at church stresses you out because you need that hour of worship with your husband in the sanctuary on Sunday mornings. Perhaps you said yes to being "room mom" in your child's preschool class, but your evenings spent cutting ladybugs out of construction paper are stealing the hours of your sleep that you desperately need these days.

Sweet friends, I promise you, there will be seasons for you to serve the Lord in many different areas! However, if you can't do those extra things, and stay calm and collected with your children at home…then maybe you need to "drop a class."

"The discerning sets his face toward wisdom, but the eyes of a fool are on the ends of the earth." (Proverbs 17:24)

Are your eyes on everything right now? Are you multitasking because you see the need for every task to be done…by you…from here to the ends of the earth? Over and over again, I rediscover one of the main themes of this little book: Be still and know. Stop the striving over multiple things and be still in the most important things. Not every child needs an extra-curricular sport every season. And you don't have to volunteer to bring snacks and crafts to every classroom party. And your teenager can learn to take the city bus. You don't need to host every Bible Study, and you don't need to throw big birthday parties. All of these things complicate, even if they do bless. And if the complicating outweighs the blessing, then it's no blessing at all!

"Better is a handful of quietness than two hands full of toil and a striving after wind." (Ecclesiastes 4:6)

Finally, one last thought about my experiences in high school and college. In my busiest times, I let fellowship with Christ and other Christians, as well as sweet time with my family, slide in lieu of everything else. Part of my healing in each overwhelmed season was reconnecting with these top priorities.

I remember, years ago, reading Stephen R. Covey's *The 7 Habits of Highly Effective People.* Listen to this pearl of wisdom: "The key is not to prioritize what's on your schedule, but to schedule your priorities."[6]

ARE YOU SO OVER-TAXED BY YOUR MULTIPLE TASKS THAT THERE'S NOTHING LEFT OVER FOR THE MOST IMPORTANT TASKS GOD HAS FOR YOU?

Our children are our priorities, and time with the Lord is the bedrock foundation that holds every aspect of our multi-faceted, multi-tasking lives together. If you are quick to lose your temper at the little priorities in your home each over-taxed day, then ask the Lord what He would have you schedule, and what you need to drop.

There are no major penalties, no huge late withdraw charges when you let the lesser things go.

Is it possible that you have said 'yes' to every seemingly urgent task? And has the stress of it all caused you to explode over your kids' disobedience, their noise, their slow arrival at the table for dinner, and their complaints when you ask them to help with the dishes? **Are you so over-taxed by your multiple tasks that there's nothing left over for the most important tasks God has for you?**

Often times I think of the words to old hymns from my youth, like this one: "Oh, what peace we often forfeit. Oh, what needless pain we bear. All because we do not carry everything to God in prayer."[7]

My sweet, multi-tasking, always-going friends, let's do that now: Take it all to the Lord in prayer.

LET'S PRAY:

"Dear Lord, is there anything You would have me drop in this season? Anything that has stressed me out and worn me thin, so that I'm all out of time to seek You, abide in You, and bear Your fruit here in my home? Abiding in You is my main

priority. And bearing Your fruit is the greatest task at hand. If there are things getting in my way, please give me Your eyes to see, Lord; Your ears to hear; and Your mind to perceive what You would have me excel in during this season, and what I need to let go of. I ask this in Jesus' name, amen."

Wendy

CHAPTER 28: TIMES OF TRANSITION

It had been two years since my husband left his career in Hollywood in an attempt to pursue an industry that was more family-friendly. When he was offered a job three hours north in a quaint beach town with a much slower pace, we believed that God was launching us into a new and happier season of blessings.

And those blessings did come—a steady income so we could provide for our family, a beautiful home near the center of town nestled against a mountainside, wonderful neighbors, and a new happy baby boy. But wouldn't you know it? The hardships far outweighed the blessings. Life-threatening illnesses, church "shopping" woes, no local family support, postpartum hormones, and my husband's long hours at work were all unforeseeable changes that we didn't exactly welcome.

The dream life I anticipated turned out to be a mere fantasy that revealed where my dependence really lay.

I had three boys under the age of 4, and though the small town was pretty, I was used to taking them to museums, indoor play facilities, mommy group play dates, and splash pads in the park. Suddenly, my world became smaller than ever, and my frustrations reached a peak. Every day, I felt overwhelmed, emotional, and stuck.

One morning, I stood in the doorway of our front porch, waving goodbye to my husband as he left for work, and my heart plummeted. I was miserable at the thought of trying to manage my two active preschoolers for the next thirteen hours while trying to nurse my fussy newborn and keep my house clean. I headed into the master bathroom to brush my teeth, and instead of the joyful, put-together woman that I thought I was, all I could see was my messy, graying hair, sagging pajama pants, and dull eyes. I looked as bad as I felt, as one suffocating day led to the next.

So my fuse shortened.
And my voice rose.
And my hope eroded.
And my heart ached.
And the kids got the brunt of it.
So my guilt swelled.

And the cycle continued as I wondered if I would ever be able to recover my gentleness and feel whole again.

I tried to get dressed more often than not, invite others over for playdates, and put together a housekeeping schedule. All of these practical things were steps in the right direction, but my frustration and irritability continued to catch me off guard. I was often exasperated over spilled milk, undone by sibling rivalry, and reactionary over disagreements with my over-worked husband.

I needed a Holy Spirit intervention.

So I put into practice two key spiritual disciplines:

1.) Quiet times of Bible reading and prayer.

And,

2.) Genuine grief and repentance over my sin, coupled with specific actions for change.

I began to protect my quiet times again. Come what may, when the kids napped, I walked past the piles of laundry, the soaking dishes, and the comfy couch. Those things could wait. I ignored the romance novel on my bedside, the TV remote, and social media. I gathered my One Year Bible, my prayer journal, and my wits, and I settled into the chair on my back porch to read and pray. Every day. I began to beg God to cleanse my heart and purify my mouth. Philippians 4:8 transformed my thinking: "Finally, brothers, whatever is true, whatever is honorable, whatever is just, whatever is pure, whatever is lovely, whatever is commendable, if there is any excellence, if there is anything worthy of praise, think about these things." I began to filter every thought through this Divine sieve.

Every time I slipped, I stopped right there and repented. And then I examined what was triggering my anger and sinful reactions. Praying for wisdom, I put a plan in place to help retrain my angry responses and I practiced, and prayed, and practiced, and prayed, and practiced, and prayed.

If I was prone to get angry over sibling rivalry, then I examined practical ways I could help them settle disputes in a peaceful manner, like giving them a fun chore they could work together on as a team. If I was impatient and spoke harshly with my kids for interrupting some meaningless thing that had my attention, then I practiced stopping mid-sentence, apologizing, and getting down on eye-level to really listen to them.

It took time—much more time than I wanted. But change happened over the course of the year.

What didn't change were my circumstances. The transition we were facing loomed as challenging as ever, and in some cases, my surroundings got even worse. What made all the difference is that I went back to the One Who never changes, and I remembered that His plans for me are ultimately good.

When you are going through change, go to the One who

never changes.

"For I the Lord do not change; therefore you, O children of Jacob, are not consumed." (Malachi 3:6)

Spending time developing my relationship with the Lord reminded me that in the midst of the dry desert or the raging storm, my Lord and Savior commands them all. I did not need to flounder under the temptation to yell at my kids or treat them with indignation because my life felt out of MY control. If we are being consumed by anything—emotions, anger, or pity-parties—then we are not relying on God and His faithful plans for our lives. We are putting our security in our circumstances, or our selfish desires to have an easier life instead of the one that God has

WHEN ALL ELSE FAILS, IF OUR FEET ARE FIRMLY PLANTED ON THE ROCK, THE LOVE OF CHRIST STEADIES OUR HEARTS AND MINDS, EVEN IF THE WHOLE EARTH GIVES WAY BENEATH US.

given to us. We have forgotten to empty ourselves for the sake of others.

During those times of change and transition, I forgot that this life is not about me and the smooth, ideal setting I wanted, so I allowed my resentment to consume me. I find a lot of hope in the fact that God is faithful, despite my lack of faith: "If we are faithless, He remains faithful— for He cannot deny Himself" (2 Timothy 2:13). I don't need to strive for the perfect solution or work harder. Peace in the midst of change comes from the knowledge that, "I can do all this through him who gives me strength." (Philippians 4:13, NIV)

If today you feel overwhelmed or in need of the stable and familiar, don't look over your shoulder at how things used to be, or into the future of what you imagine life could become. Look to God, Who never takes His eyes off of you. Ask the Lord to carry you through THIS moment, in this home, with these people. **When all else fails, if our feet are firmly planted on the Rock, the love of Christ steadies our hearts and minds, even if the whole earth gives way beneath us.** God knows the number of hairs on our heads and He knows the challenges we are facing. Nothing about the path you are on is permitted without His loving consent. Trust that God is in the transition as much as He was before your world turned topsy-turvy. Have the courage to believe that it can even be for your GOOD.

"Therefore, my dear brothers and sisters, stand firm. Let nothing move you. Always give yourselves fully to the work of the Lord, because you know that your labor in the Lord is not in vain." (1 Corinthians 15:58)

Eventually, we would face yet another big move and even more challenging transitions. I believe that, as long as we live in this world, we will face change that often unnerves us; but it doesn't have to make us into discontented and heated moms. Allow these times of change to refine you, and know that today is a day that you can have victory—not because everything is as you wish, but because God, in His care for you, is unaltered and true.

LET'S PRAY:

"Father, You are the same yesterday, today, and forever. I know that this time of transition is not a surprise to You and that You have allowed me to face these changes. You are with me in the midst of uncertainty. I know that in this chapter of my life where everything seems unsettled that You remain steady. I need Your help to feel secure and at peace in my circumstances simply because I am Your child and You are my loving Father. I don't want to be irritable or complain, nor do I want to let my emotions rule my heart and mouth. Give me more of Your Holy Spirit in my life and help me to be unflappable, resilient, and victorious! Thank You for being my Rock and my firm foundation! In Jesus' name, amen!

Amber

CHAPTER 29: CARING FOR SICK CHILDREN AND AILING PARENTS

I have a friend whose child has been in and out of the hospital with multiple undiagnosed genetic abnormalities. Doctors don't even know how to label her illness. But my girlfriend...she can label it all with one short word: HARD. It's hard. And it's sad. And it's faith building. And it's anger making. And it's been going on longer than they'd ever imagined, with still no end in sight.

There are long stretches of dark night when Allyson cares for her girl, fevered and retching from the pain. Amidst the suffering, this dear mom is not only nursemaid to her daughter, she is therapist, preacher, cheerleader, and prayer warrior, too. She is her child's most faithful advocate on earth, fighting for her educational and medical needs, and can be a fierce lioness when negotiating insurance coverage. There are trips to the emergency room that are suddenly transformed into weeks in an intensive care unit, where my friend stays by her daughter's side through most every day and night. All the while, there are other children missing her at home.

Groceries need buying, dinners need making, dirty clothes

need washing, and the little healthy people are desperate for a present, loving mom as well. And the burden seems too big to carry most days. And yet, amidst the impossible weight of it all, Allyson has found a joy, a strength, an eternal perspective that can only come supernaturally, through the power of God's Holy Spirit.

"O God, I believe that in the darkness You are brewing light, that in the storm clouds You are gathering sunshine, that in the mines You are fashioning diamonds, and in the beds of the sea You are making pearls. I believe that however unfathomable may be Your designs, yet they have a bottom. Though it is in the whirlwind and in the storm, You have a way that is good and righteous altogether."[8] — Charles Spurgeon

Allyson keeps a private blog going, so that family members and loved ones can stay abreast and know how to best pray for this sweet family. She often shares stories of her daughter's tenacious faith and hope. That little girl has become an inspiration to all who know her and read of her enduring trust in God. She has lived many years in the fiery furnace of her illness, but has come forth as gold refined. And so has her mother. *Unfortunately, the refinement has not been in the form of physical healing, but spiritual wholeness and health.*

I have never had a grievously ill child, nor have I been the long-term caregiver of an ailing parent, but I have known enough of these everyday servants to learn that the beauty God brings from these ashes often has more to do with our hearts than their bodies. Though we pray for God to heal and transform our sick family member, often times the healing and transformation has more to do with our heart's transformation.

I know another woman who endured long months with her premature baby, only to experience the inconceivable pain of losing a child a few months after a difficult birth. She confessed to me how she struggled to be present and tender with the children who had survived their baby brother. She knew, intellectually, that her deepest desire was to love well the living children in her midst, but the grief and exhaustion of the previous months, as her child fought for his life in the NICU, had weighed her down and nearly broken her. She was short-tempered, raised her voice, and even used cuss words in their home. She was broken, snapping under the pressure of her grief. But through it all, she clung tearfully to the promise that God would again turn her mourning into dancing, if she would obediently abide in His comfort and goodness.

It was in this broken obedience, in this persevering place, that my friend recognized that grief swaddled in exhaustion had become her trigger. And I imagine she is not alone in this reality. I bet there are many of you reading through this collection of triggers, who are likewise in a constant state of on-going care as you minister to the sick ones in your life. Your grandpa with dementia, your child with Leukemia, your sister going through another round of Chemo for her aggressive breast cancer, your mother with her hip replacement surgery after another fall.

THE GREAT PHYSICIAN SOMETIMES CHOOSES TO HEAL OUR LOVED ONES, AND OTHER TIMES USES THEIR ILLNESS TO HEAL US.

It all lies upon your heart and your weary skin like death and sadness. And while you want to be able to flip the switch when it's time to engage with your healthy, happy people, it's just not that simple. And so the trigger inappropriately fires at the wrong time, sending a canopy of arrows at your children. And the tears flow hot again.

While I would love to give you a simple prayer to pray that will instantaneously soothe your nerves, heal your loved ones, and correct your misplaced anger, I can't. But I can point you back again and again and again to the One who is sovereign and purposeful over all. **The Great Physician sometimes chooses to heal our loved ones, and other times uses their illness to heal us.** It is my prayer for you, if this is where you are living right now, taking care of sick children or ailing parents, that you would avail your own heart of the healing He has made available to you through Christ.

Sometimes the healing comes in like a constant IV drip through the comforting nearness of the Holy Spirit; other times, it's administered in the stolen moments where we seek God in His Word; and still other times, we find healing as we learn new parenting tools to use in the midst of our most stressful seasons.

My friend who lost her infant son learned to communicate in a healthier way with her children and her husband during their darkest days. She called a family meeting, the first of many that would follow, and in the safety of their living room apologized for her behavior. She confessed her heartbreak and her weariness, and then repented for the way she had been taking her grief out on the family. She acknowledged that they were grieving, too; the loss of a brother and even a mother, during those long months when she practically lived at the hospital. She asked for their forgiveness, and they were quick to give it.

And she clung to God's promise that she would surely see the goodness of the Lord again, right there in the land of the living. Her living children and her living hope in the Living God, Who cares so much about our healing.

LET'S PRAY:

"Dear Lord, I cling to You in every storm, in the midst of every dark night, when illness and fear threaten to undo me, I trust in You! Every hour, every need, every pain, every diagnoses, every loss, every sleepless night, every seemingly unanswered prayer. I trust You, again and again. Though I don't always understand why You've allowed so much suffering, I do know that it is in the blackest night, that Your Morning Star shines the brightest. You are shining in my life, Lord, and in the lives of my loved ones. I praise You, Lord. Amen."

Wendy

CHAPTER 30: STRESS

•••

Stress: noun

a state of mental or emotional strain or tension resulting from adverse or very demanding circumstances: "he's obviously under a lot of stress"

synonyms: strain, pressure, worry, anxiety[9]

One of the most common causes of mommy-anger can be summed up with this one, monosyllabic word: stress. At its root, it often has nothing to do with our kids' childish behavior, and everything to do with the difficult challenges in our lives that have brought us to this breaking point.

Stress.

I think of the old adage, "the straw that broke the camel's back." Isn't that often what we break over? That small thing that finally sends us over the edge. The noise they make, the way they whine, dazing off into space rather than grabbing their shoes when we're running late. The straw that suddenly makes all the weight unbearable!

Some stressors are huge! Divorce mediations are coming up and the children don't want to see their dad for his visitations; the school keeps calling because of your child's behavior, and they want him tested for every disorder known to man; your in-laws don't invite you over, but they do spend time with all their other children and grandchildren; money is tight and there's no end in sight; your back is carrying physical stress too, and you can't get into the doctor because there's no one to help you with the kids! Stress. Stress! Enormous STRESS!!!

Stress literally means "pressure." And pressure weighs heavy upon us like a physical weight. And sometimes the weight is simply too much, and you break. But God has a cure for the heavy burdens we carry. No, more than that—He is the cure.

"Come to me, all you who are weary and burdened, and I will give you rest. Take my yoke upon you and learn from me, for I am gentle and humble in heart, and you will find rest for your souls. For my yoke is easy and my burden is light." (Matthew 11:28-30, NIV)

I'm tenderhearted towards you, sweet ladies, as I punch these keys down and quote a Bible verse that you believe in your head, but can't make yourself experience in the middle of all the pressure you're under. You cry out for Him, I know you do, and you believe that He hears you in your distress. You ask Him to carry your burdens, and believe fresh again that He wants you to walk in His peace. But then the next moment comes upon you hard and heavy, and immediately you are weighed down again.

What words do I have to offer you when true relief seems so far away? Only one: FAITH.

Faith is believing…even when there's no end in sight.
Faith is the antidote to fear.
Faith is the antidote to worry.
Faith is the antidote to stress.
Faith is the antidote to every demon breathing sulfuric lies down the back of your neck..
Faith… is the key to it all.

> *"Do not worry then, saying, 'What will we eat?' or 'What will we drink?' or 'What will we wear for clothing?' For the Gentiles eagerly seek all these things; for your heavenly Father knows that you need all these things. But seek first His kingdom and His righteousness, and all these things will be added to you. So do not worry about tomorrow; for tomorrow will care for itself. Each day has enough trouble of its own." (Matthew 6:31-34, NASB)*

The key is faith: believing that the Lord knows all your needs, in the midst of these refining fires. The furnace of faith, hot and holy, is the place God meets us. Ministering to us in the flames. And maybe, just maybe, you need to rededicate yourself to unwavering faith in Christ today. Right now. Saying, "Lord, I've been crying out to You for help, but not really believing that You will do it. I do believe, help me in my unbelief. I choose again and again to believe that You are able to handle all that concerns me today. Amen."

When we believe that He is able, He transforms our stress into surrender. Remember, when we glance at God's strong promises with enough frequency, we won't be glancing anymore – but gazing without end. Our eyes will be forever fixed upon Him and His ability to handle everything that comes our way.

If stress has been your trigger, causing you to snap, and you have passed the stress onto your children, then it's time to repent. To repent literally means to turn around, do a complete 180, and walk the other way. If you have gotten yourself into a stressed-out place, where all you can do is heap the same burdens upon the small backs of your beloveds, it's time to use the muscle of your heart and knock it off. It's time to stop it, turn around, and follow Jesus the right way! Here at the end of this book that has been laced in grace, I'm speaking firm words.

If you have believed, and asked Jesus to save you from your sin, you are free—but you are not free to keep on sinning. You have been bought with a costly price. Jesus' blood literally ran out of His body to atone for your stressed-out sin tendencies. He has saved you, and is eager to transform you—to change you from an angry mom into a pleasant woman of peace and patience.

"What shall we say, then? Shall we go on sinning so that grace may increase? By no means! We died to sin; how can we live in it any longer?" (Romans 6:1-2, NIV)

If you have made it this far in your reading, then I know, dear heart, that you do not want to go on sinning any longer! Praise God for that. His Word tells us that, "No one born of God makes a practice of sinning, for God's seed abides in him, and he cannot keep on sinning because he has been born of God." (1 John 3:9)

When each of my children put their faith in Christ and asked to be baptized, we would ask them why they wanted to be baptized. Each little Christian would simply say, "I want to show everyone that I'm following Jesus!" And that's what we're doing here and now. We are recommitting to follow Jesus. By the power of His Holy Spirit at work in our lives, we are choosing to turn from our sin, and follow hard after Jesus in the opposite

IF YOU HAVE BELIEVED, AND ASKED JESUS TO SAVE YOU FROM YOUR SIN, YOU ARE FREE—BUT YOU ARE NOT FREE TO KEEP ON SINNING.

direction.

If you have hurt your family with your stressed screams and anxious accusations, and impressed upon them the pressures you bear, then it is time to stop. It is time to stop. It is time to apologize to your loved ones when you are calm. And it's time to make a plan that will carry you down the right side of the road—going the right way with your children—following Jesus in the way you live and the words you speak and the tone you use. Repent and render yourself this day dead to sin, but alive to righteousness!

> *"Even so consider yourselves to be dead to sin, but alive to God in Christ Jesus. Therefore do not let sin reign in your mortal body so that you obey its lusts, and do not go on presenting the members of your body to sin as instruments of unrighteousness; but present yourselves to God as those alive from the dead, and your members as instruments of righteousness to God." (Romans 6:11-13, NASB)*

> *"The night is nearly over; the day is almost here. So let us put aside the deeds of darkness and put on the armor of light." (Romans 13:12, NIV)*

LET'S PRAY:

"Dear Lord, I want to follow hard after you! Direct my

footsteps according to Your word; let no sin rule over me. (Psalm 119:133) Sin is no longer my master, because I am not under the law, but under grace. (Romans 6:14) Give me Your strength, and the convicting nearness of Your Holy Spirit to remind me of what is right when I am tempted to do wrong. Protect me from the evil one who delights in my sin. Give me the courage to proclaim, "Satan, get behind me" when I hear him whisper lies. I am not his and his ways are not mine. I am Yours, Jesus, over and over again Yours. So I am following You! Amen."

Wendy

CHAPTER 31: FEELINGS OF GUILT

....

I had just washed Rosey, our black lab puppy, to shiny perfection, when she slipped from my grip and ran straight for the mud again. As my mouth dropped in horror, she pranced gleefully, mud spattering all over her freshly shampooed coat.

I sighed.

We moms who struggle with guilty feelings are a lot like puppies who run back into the mud. We may know that, in theory, we are washed and clean by the blood of Jesus; but we feel like we are still slathered in the mire and the muck of our sin. We allow the weight and memory of our guiltiness to figuratively splatter our hearts with clods of dirt and filth. It's hard to embrace that we are fully clean!

Some of us feel overwhelmed in our struggle with anger and yelling. Our guilt breaks our hearts and our shame hangs heavily over our shoulders like an ill-fitting coat. It's a challenge to think of ourselves as anything else but failures. But that's not who we really are or how we should be thinking.

Every guilty mom needs to remember two things:

1.) God has a plan for your life.

And,

2.) Satan has a plan for your life.

One of the most well known verses in the Bible is one of great encouragement from Jeremiah 29:11, "For I know the plans I have for you," declares the Lord, "plans to prosper you and not to harm you, plans to give you hope and a future." Although God is speaking to His people in captivity in this passage, it reveals the loving heart of God. We are further reassured in Romans 8:28, "And we know that for those who love God all things work together for good, for those who are called according to his purpose." All throughout the Bible, we see that Jesus loved us and gave Himself for us, and that He is intimately and providentially *for us.*

On the other hand, our enemy has a plan for us, too. 1 Peter 5:8 warns us, "Be sober-minded; be watchful. Your adversary the devil prowls around like a roaring lion, seeking someone to devour." For the mom who struggles with anger and keeping watch over her mouth, his tactic is to defeat us in the battlefield of our minds. If the Devil can disarm us by discouraging us over our sin, then he can conquer not just our own assurance of worth in Christ, but can also do damage in our homes. His goal is to devour us, and if he can do so by making us useless for Christ in the lives of our children and convincing us that we cannot be victorious over the sin that so easily entangles us, then he wins.

> *"The thief comes only to steal and kill and destroy. I came that they may have life and have it abundantly." (John 10:10)*

Satan's plan is to steal, kill, and destroy your life.

Jesus' plan is to give you life—life to the full.

The ultimate question for you is simple: **Whose plan will you follow?**

●●●●●●●●●●●●●●●●●●●●●●●●●●●●●●●●●●●●●●

GUILT DEFEATS. CONVICTION CATAPULTS-TOWARDS SPIRITUAL GROWTH AND FREEDOM!

●●●●●●●●●●●●●●●●●●●●●●●●●●●●●●●●●●●●●●

Satan loves to play D.J. in our minds, playing records of lies. He sashays close with the thought that it's too late —we've already ruined our kids by our furious reactions. He waltzes into our hearts and tells us that we can never change. He two-steps into our thoughts at night as we lay awake comparing ourselves to "better moms." *But we must not dance with the Devil.*

There is a big difference between guilt and conviction. One is meant to condemn you, the other to free you.

How do you know if you are feeling an unhealthy guilt versus a righteous conviction? **Guilt defeats. Conviction catapults—towards spiritual growth and freedom!**

God always convicts us with a loving reproach that causes us to want to keep going in His strength and not in our own flesh. It moves us forward toward growth in our spiritual lives, instead of backwards or inwards towards discouragement.

For those of us that love God, we are already rescued from the grip of sin and guilt. Look at what God says about those of us who are saved by the atoning work of Jesus Christ on the cross:

> *"There is therefore now no condemnation for those who are in Christ Jesus. For the law of the life-giving Spirit in Christ Jesus has set you free from the law of sin and death." (Romans 8:1-2)*

> *"For he has rescued us from the dominion of darkness and brought us into the kingdom of the Son he*

loves." (Colossians 1:13, NIV)

"So if the Son sets you free, you will be free indeed." (John 8:36)

These verses breathe life and hope into the heart of the believer! Not crushing condemnation! If God no longer condemns us, why must we condemn ourselves? That's not really even logical, is it? Satan has fine-tuned his tactics over the course of history, and he is good at telling us lies and condemning both us and our kids through guilty feelings; but that is not living life to the full!

Is God convicting you of your anger issues?

Do you feel a need to change and a desire to keep pursuing God?

After reading through this book for the last 31 days, is there a spark of hope in your heart that you really can be transformed?

Then you are on the right track! Keep running the race! But don't let your nasty enemy, the Devil, tell you that you will never change, that your kids are too damaged, or that you are a failure. God would never say that about you! As author Alan Fadling says, those thoughts sound much more like an enemy than a friend! And that's exactly who is feeding them to you.[10]

In Christ, you are clean and forgiven. He loves you and me as much in this moment as in any other. He loves us when we are overcoming temptation and He loves us when we yield to it. He loves us too much to let us continue down any wrong path, but He does not stand at the end as our accuser. We must not roll around in the dirt of sin any longer, coating ourselves with the very darkness that Jesus died to wash away. See yourself as God sees you: cleansed in Jesus' blood, and without spot or wrinkle. Live life to the full as God intended, *one opportunity to overcome your triggers at a time*, and watch as God transforms you moment by moment, from an angry mom to one who embodies a gentle and graceful spirit.

Go into today, and tomorrow, with the peace of Christ who loved you and gave Himself for you, and lay down your burden of guilt at the foot of the cross where it belongs. Leave it there, along with your triggers, and live free.

LET'S PRAY:

"Dear Father, You sent Your Son to die on the cross for my sins. I am clean and forgiven. You do not condemn me. Thank You, Jesus, for coming to give me life to the full! I need Your peace and assurance that I am free from the guilt of my sin!

Keep Satan away from me, so that he is not able to whisper lies to me any longer. Help me to capture my thoughts and dwell on what is true and right, and help me to feel Your pleasure. Forgive me for my sinful anger, and help me to live my life in the knowledge of Your grace. Protect my mind; help me to see myself and my children as You see us, and give me joy. Lord, I turn from my angry ways, knowing that You will transform me from this day forward! I trust that You can make something beautiful out of my life, and my relationship with my children, too. Thank You! In Jesus Name, amen!

Amber

EPILOGUE: COMMENCEMENT

I tried to find the right word for the title of this chapter. In reality, this is the book's epilogue. 'Epi-' is the Greek root for *after*, and '-logue' means *words*. These are, quite literally, the words that come after our words. And isn't that what's most important? What we do and say after these words have all been read?

Which made me think of graduation celebrations. Commencement literally means "beginning." As a child, I thought that commencement was a party celebrating the end; but really, one thing has to end before a whole new thing can start. And so this is our commencement celebration—the end of our natural, sinful reactions and the start of righteous, biblical responses. This is our new beginning, and our send off into a right way of responding, rather than reacting, to the people in our midst.

> *"I have been crucified with Christ. It is no longer I who live, but Christ who lives in me. And the life I now live in the flesh I live by faith in the Son of God, who loved me and gave himself for me." (Galatians 2:20)*

> *"Therefore, if anyone is in Christ, he is a new creation.*

253

The old has passed away; behold, the new has come." (2 Corinthians 5:17)

This is not to say that you, my dearly loved "new creation," won't make a mothering mistake. You will. But in this new dawn, here at the beginning of our new day, we have the Holy Spirit's convicting nearness and the God-strength to stop and ask ourselves, "What would Jesus have me to do in this parenting moment? Which way is He going? Do I need to repent, turn around, and go the other way?" For if He truly is residing in us, in our days, in our mothering moments, then He is available to lead us from within as we chase after His righteousness...even when our fleshly buttons are being pushed and our natural triggers are threatening to fire inappropriately.

It is because of His gracious Spirit, who abides in us and bids us abide in Him, that we are able to bear the fruit of His Spirit in our lives: Love, Joy, Peace, Patience, Kindness, Goodness, Gentleness, Faithfulness, and Self-Control. And so we begin at the beginning, abiding at the start of each new day. Rousing, if possible, before our children do. Leaning into grace each new day, that we might extend grace to those within our homes.

Likewise, we praise God continually, for we are the recipients of forgiveness—and so we offer that to our beloveds as well. How often? Not once each new day, but multiple times, over and over again, all day long, tiring as it may be. We call this perseverance, endurance, pressing on.

> *"I press on so that I may lay hold of that for which also I was laid hold of by Christ Jesus. Brethren, I do not regard myself as having laid hold of it yet; but one thing I do: forgetting what lies behind and reaching forward to what lies ahead, I press on toward the goal for the prize of the upward call of God in Christ Jesus." (Philippians 3:12-14, NASB)*

And so today, with pomp and circumstance playing on these last pages, let us remember that this parenting gig is a marathon and not a sprint. Pace yourself by keeping pace with the Spirit. This is your commencement charge: Press into Him at the beginning of each new day, and press on!

Pressing on in Christ is where the shackles of generational sin begin to lose their grip. Bitterness and exhaustion fall at His feet. Hearts of stone begin to soften into hearts of flesh as we press on. We are not the tail end of our parents' generational curse, but the head of a righteous, new line. **As a new creation, you are not defined by the life you have lived, but liberated to live new life!**

It seems to me, here on the precipice of a brand-new way of communicating with our loved ones in our homes, that within each new day, we have been gifted a myriad of sacred moments. We used to call them triggers. Triggered to blame and shame. But now, they are simply opportunities to commit again to righteousness one holy moment, one holy choice, at a time.

TRIGGERS = OPPORTUNITIES

What will I do when my child throws a tantrum? What will I say when my children talk back? How will I respond when I'm ignored? What plans will I make to help me through long evenings when I'm parenting alone, when my nerves are shot and my load is too heavy? How will I respond when I'm overwhelmed by my child's ADHD, my husband's lack of involvement, and my MIL's seemingly judgmental remarks? What will I do when I'm up to my neck in difficult transitions, when change is the last thing I need?

What will I do with all these opportunities? Will I let them drive me far from my God and His holiness, or let them be the impetus to draw near to Him and His righteousness? These are the questions we ask ourselves when each new morning's mercy is still wet like dew upon the ground. What will I do today? Will I remain stuck in patterns of yesterday, or eagerly believe that new things are possible and springing forth?

> *"Remember not the former things, nor consider the things of old. Behold, I am doing a new thing; now it*

springs forth, do you not perceive it? I will make a way in the wilderness and rivers in the desert." (Isaiah 43:18-19)

Wendy

ACKNOWLEDGEMENTS

Amber Lia:

My Knights—I have been praying for you beautiful boys since I was a young girl myself. One of the reasons I know God loves me is because He gave me you. If in this lifetime, I achieve only one thing that qualifies me to hear the words, "Well done, good and faithful servant," I want it to be because of the godly way I mothered you precious boys. I love you all, acres and oceans and buckets and barrels full!

Oliver, you are my strong, talented, and bright leader! We are buddies—I'm so proud to have you as my friend. Your passion for the Lord shines brightly and is a testimony to everyone who knows you—may it always be so, my angel cake.

Quinn, your joyful and happy heart makes me smile! And those freckles? Icing on the cake. Your sensitive spirit and empathy towards others is a continual reminder to me of the love of Jesus in your life. Thank you for being an example to me, love bucket.

Oakley, you are a constant ray of sunshine! You are quick to love and forgive. I'm pretty sure you don't have a mean bone in your body and you make parenting a breeze. I'm so glad God gave me my own personal class clown! God has big plans for your life, and I'm on the edge of my seat to see how He takes your pure heart and uses it for His glory, you sweet lamb.

Guy, you are the one who encouraged me to write from the very beginning. This book, ultimately, is because of you. Thank you for giving up so much of your own personal time so that I could pour my heart out on paper and follow my calling. I'm my best self when I'm partnering with you—in parenting and in life. You believe in this message of grace-filled parenting and you live it out with me in our home. I could never have dreamed up a better father for our boys. I love you!

Mom and Dad, you gave me the best gift a parent could give —the foundation of the Word of God that transformed me and set the course of my life. I'm so deeply grateful for you both! I love you.

My agent, *Janet Grant*, thank you for giving me your blessing on this project and for always championing my writing!

And *Wendy*, how could I have known when I "met" you on

the phone just a couple years ago now, that you would be so instrumental in my life? This process of writing something so close to my heart became even more precious because of you. Your words inspire, uplift, and encourage me over and over again. To minister with you has been a highlight of my life. Thank you for making this writing process an absolute joy! I love you, sister.

Wendy Speake:

Mom - Your tender and supportive mothering, along with your phenomenal grandmothering, are two of the obvious blessings in my life. However, it is your consistent availability to help me with my boys that alleviates many of my personal stressors. In essence, you soothe my *Triggers*. You have been one of God's greatest gifts to me—and now to my children.

Dad - Your calm and even-tempered parenting, your commitment to spend time with us growing up, and the way you led us faithfully to church each Sunday were foundational blessings in my growing-up years. I love you. And I know that you love me very much.

Matt - There is no one on this planet I would rather figure this parenting thing out with. I am forever amazed by the man that you continue to grow into. You are a walking, talking testimony of God's ongoing work in a believer's life. (And you aren't hard on the eyes, either!) Thank you for always setting an example for the boys and me of a life spent seeking the Lord.

Caleb, Brody, and Asher - God did such a good job when He made each one of you!

Caleb, you are independent, confident, and kind. You are a wonderful musician, a faithful friend, and a dynamite big brother. You pursue the Lord with all of your heart, unashamed, and inspire me to do the same.

Brody, you are a ray of sunshine! Your creativity and humor sparkle and shine, and everyone around you is blessed. Your faith is tender and deep, and I can't wait to see all that the Lord has planned for you.

Asher, you are both the smallest and the biggest in our home. You are my little man, so eager to flex your muscles—physically and spiritually. Your passion for life and love is enormous!

Amber Lia - The Lord put us together for such a time as this… I have no doubt. And yet, sweet friend, I hope and pray that He has other plans for other times. Here's to our friendship—may it last for an eternity.

NOTES

NOTES

● ●

[1] "What Does the Bible Say about Respect?" GotQuestions.org. Got Questions Ministries. Web. 1 Dec. 2015. <http://www.gotquestions.org/Bible-respect.html>.

[2] MacArthur, John F., *Ephesians MacArthur New Testament Commentary*, (Chicago, IL: Moody Press, 1986), 317.

[3] Priolo, Lou, *The Heart of Anger* (Amityville, NY: Calvary Press, 1997), 127.

[4] Thomas, Gary, *Sacred Marriage* (Grand Rapids, MI: Zondervan, 2000).

[5] Frost, Robert. "Mending Wall." Tendencies in Modern American Poetry. New York: Macmillan Co., 1920. Gleeditions. Web. 1 Dec. 2015. < http://gleeditions.com/mendingwall/students/pages.asp?pg=5>

[6] Covey, Stephen R., *The 7 Habits of Highly Effective People* (N.Y., N.Y.: Simon and Schuster, 1989), 170.

[7] Scriven, Joseph, "What a Friend We Have in Jesus", (1855).

[8] Spurgeon, Charles, *The Complete Sermons of C. H. Spurgeon, Book 1* (Harrington, DE: Delmarva Publications Inc.) 140.

[9] "Stress 1." Stress: Definition of Stress in Oxford Dictionary (American English) (US). Oxford University Press. Web. 1 Dec. 2015. < http://www.oxforddictionaries.com/us/definition/american_english/stress>

[10] Fadling, Alan, *An Unhurried Life: Following Jesus' Rhythms of Work and Rest* (Downers Grove, IL: Intervarsity Press, 2013).

TRIGGERS STUDY GUIDE

••

You've seen a need for change in your life and you're ready to embark on the journey away from reactionary, quick-tempered parenting. But the path ahead can seem daunting and lonely without a guide or friend to walk with you. That's why authors, Amber Lia and Wendy Speake have created this in-depth study guide to accompany their book, *Triggers: Exchanging Parents' Angry Reactions for Gentle Biblical Responses.* Perfect for individual reflection or a group study setting, this resource features a come-alongside approach to working through external and internal triggers that fuel your struggle with anger. Mirroring the 31-chapter structure of Triggers, this study guide will provide you with:

- Rich passages of Scripture to meditate on and tuck into your heart for strength.

- Expanded thoughts on each trigger for further teaching and encouragement.

- Questions to spark personal reflection and to help move you toward action.

- Plenty of room to write out your thoughts and work through the chapter questions.

- Additional space for doodling, writing out prayers or action plans, and more!

If you're seeking real transformation in your parenting and you're willing to do the work to get there — this study guide will equip, empower, and encourage you along the way!

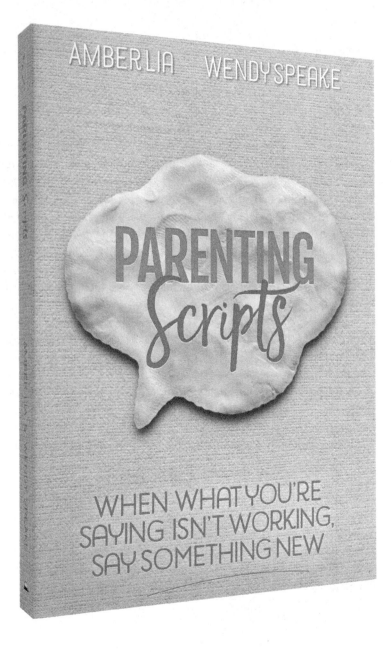

PARENTING SCRIPTS

••

You want to say the right thing when your children do wrong — trouble is most parents aren't sure where to even begin. *Parenting Scripts* is the much-needed resource for moms and dads who are desperate to speak life to their children instead of defaulting to the same old words and ineffective consequences. Focusing on the most ordinary and yet troublesome areas in our daily routines, *Parenting Scripts* helps parents to craft intentional, well thought out and prayed over words.

When parents step back to consider their children's wrong actions, there's a chance they can plan the right reactions. In the margins of their busy day, *Parenting Scripts* leads parents to a calm place where they can pinpoint their family's bad habits and choose better ways of dealing with immature behavior — theirs and their children's.

Laid out as a parenting book and workbook all in one, each of the thirty-one short chapters includes:

• Parenting Script — main lesson, complete with a script to try at home

• Scriptures — verses to apply

• Prayer Script — prayer to pray

• Make the Script Your Own — empty page to write down your own parenting script

Made in the USA
Coppell, TX
05 November 2019